HENRY VII

Henry VII
THIRD EDITION

ROGER LOCKYER
and
ANDREW THRUSH

LONGMAN
LONDON AND NEW YORK

Addison Wesley Longman Limited
Edinburgh Gate
Harlow, Essex CM20 2JE
England
and Associated Companies throughout the world.

Published in the United States of America
by Addison Wesley Longman Inc., New York

First published 1968
Second edition 1983
Third edition 1997

ISBN 0 582 20912 9 PPR

British Library Cataloguing in Publication Data

A catalogue record for this book is
available from the British Library

Library of Congress Cataloging-in-Publication Data

Lockyer, Roger.
Henry VII / Roger Lockyer and Andrew Thrush. -- 3rd ed.
    p. cm. -- (Seminar studies in history)
  Includes bibliographical references and index.
  ISBN 0-582-20912-9 (alk. paper)
  1. Great Britain--Politics and government--1485–1509.
  2. Finance, Public--Great Britain--To 1688.
  3. Great Britain--History--Henry VII, 1485–1509.
  I. Thrush, Andrew. II. Title. III. Series.
JN181.L63 1997
942.05'1--dc20   96-38692
                                                                        CIP

Set by 7 in 10/12 Sabon
Produced through Longman Malaysia, VVP

CONTENTS

EDITORIAL FOREWORD

Such is the pace of historical enquiry in the modern world that there is an ever-widening gap between the specialist article or monograph, incorporating the results of current research, and general surveys, which inevitably become out of date. *Seminar Studies in History* are designed to bridge this gap. The books are written by experts in their field who are not only familiar with the latest research but have often contributed to it. They are frequently revised, in order to take account of new information and interpretations. They provide a selection of documents to illustrate major themes and provoke discussion, and also a guide to further reading. Their aim is to clarify complex issues without over-simplifying them, and to stimulate readers into deepening their knowledge and understanding of major themes and topics.

NOTE ON REFERENCING SYSTEM

Readers should note that numbers in square brackets [5] refer them to the corresponding entry in the Bibliography at the end of the book (specific page numbers are given in italics). A number in square brackets preceded by *Doc.* [*Doc. 5*] refers readers to the corresponding item in the Documents section which follows the main text.

PREFACE TO THE SECOND EDITION

The first edition of this Seminar Study was published in 1968, but since that time a great deal of work has been done on the Yorkist and early Tudor period, and many of the interpretations put forward in the first edition are no longer tenable. This second edition, therefore, is not so much a revision of the earlier text as a complete rewriting. It contains a number of new sections, such as those on 'The Common Law and Chancery' and 'The Church'. It also omits the sections on 'The machinery of government' and 'The weakness of the Crown' which appeared in the earlier version. The main reason for this is the addition to the Seminar Studies Series of David Cook's study of *Lancastrians and Yorkists: The Wars of the Roses*, which deals with the half-century preceding Henry VII's accession.

ROGER LOCKYER, 1982

PREFACE TO THE THIRD EDITION

Since the publication of the second edition of this Seminar Study the pace of research into the early Tudor period has not slackened, and many interpretations formerly taken for granted have now had to be revised. There is not always agreement on what to put in their place, and this third edition of *Henry VII* should therefore be regarded as, in certain respects, an interim report on a continuing debate. We decided to drop the brief section on 'Rural and Urban Society' which opened the 'Background' section of previous editions in order to devote more space to the crucial chapters on Henrician finance and government, which have been completely rewritten, as has the chapter on Henry's foreign policy. The Documents section has also been expanded. This third edition is the joint work of Roger Lockyer and his former student and colleague, Dr Andrew Thrush, who has made it his objective to keep abreast of the latest work on the first Tudor.

ROGER LOCKYER & ANDREW THRUSH, 1996

ACKNOWLEDGEMENTS

The publishers would like to thank the following for permission to reproduce copyright material: The Royal Historical Society for extracts from Camden Third Series, Vol. LXXIV, *The Anglica Historia 1485–1537* by Polydore Vergil, edited and translated by Denys Hay; The Selden Society for extracts from *Select Cases in the Council of Henry VII*, by C.G. Baynes; Extracts from the *Calendar of the Close Rolls Henry VII*, Vol. II 1500–1509 and *Statutes of the Realm*. Crown copyright is reproduced with the permission of the Controller of Her Majesty's Stationery Office.

PART ONE: THE BACKGROUND

1 THE YORKIST INHERITANCE

In 1399 Henry Bolingbroke, Duke of Lancaster, deposed Richard II and seized the throne for himself. Although he thereby established the House of Lancaster as the ruling dynasty he had set an example that other ambitious magnates would one day follow, with fateful consequences for his descendants. The second Lancastrian monarch, Henry V, who succeeded his father in 1413, won prestige for himself and his dynasty by reasserting the old claim to France, taking an army across the Channel, and winning a resounding victory at Agincourt in 1415. But Henry V died in 1422, leaving as heir a baby son. A minority was always a dangerous time for a dynasty, particularly one so recently established, but the magnates who surrounded the infant Henry VI behaved with remarkable restraint and protected his inheritance.

It was only when Henry came of age that things started to go badly wrong. One reason for this was that the early triumphs in France had given way to defeats, and the financial strain of maintaining the English armies there was causing unrest at home. Another, and more important, reason was Henry's singular lack of the qualities needed to make a successful ruler. He was too easily swayed by those around him, and open-handed to the point of irresponsibility. By giving away royal lands and patronage to those he favoured, he blew into flames the smouldering jealousies among the magnates and thereby precipitated violent quarrels between them that he proved unable to resolve [31; 33]. Henry's incapacity and occasional relapses into insanity intensified rivalry among the leading nobles and led directly to the conflicts between them that became known as the Wars of the Roses. The only possible outcome to these, other than stalemate, was the triumph of one of the magnate factions, and this came about in March 1461 when Edward, Duke of York, destroyed the Lancastrian army at Towton in Yorkshire. Just over a year later he was crowned king as Edward IV.

THE GOVERNMENT OF THE REALM

Edward IV was not yet twenty when he became king, and the energy which he derived from his strong physique was reinforced by his determination to be a strong ruler. He had many of the qualities needed for success. He won men to him by his charm and easy manners, while women found his good looks irresistible, but he was no mere playboy. He had a keen business sense, he could be ruthless in the pursuit of his objectives, and he was resolved to restore the royal authority [34].

The change of ruler had an immediate effect upon the Council, which was the principal instrument of royal government. Under Henry VI it had been a virtually autonomous body, dominated by the magnates, and Sir John Fortescue, who had served as Chief Justice under Henry VI, accurately summarised its weaknesses: 'The King's Council was wont to be chosen of great princes, and of the greatest lords of the land, both spiritual and temporal, and also of other men that were in great authority and offices. Which lords and officers had at hand also many matters of their own to be treated in the Council, as had the King. Wherethrough, when they came together, they were so occupied with their own matters and with the matters of their kin, servants and tenants, that they attended but little, and otherwhile nothing, to the King's matters' [11 *p. 145*]. Edward rapidly changed this state of affairs. He did not exclude magnates from the Council if he thought he could depend on their loyalty, but he did not allow them to dominate it, and he insisted that they should attend to his business rather than their own.

In the second half of Edward's reign, post-1471, there were some twenty noble Councillors, but many of these were Yorkist creations, and as a group they were smaller than the clerics, who numbered about thirty-five [27]. Clerics had always played a major part in medieval government because they were literate, they could be rewarded for service to the crown by promotion in the Church, and they left no legitimate heirs to claim a hereditary right to advise the King. Under Edward, as under his predecessors, churchmen occupied major offices of state such as the Lord Chancellorship, but the episcopate was no longer the preserve of the aristocracy. Edward tended to choose as bishops men who came from lesser gentry or merchant families and were therefore dependent on royal favour for their advancement [34].

Much the same was true of the third group of Councillors, consisting mainly of officials of the royal household, which numbered eleven in the first half of the reign but increased to twenty-three post-1471 – a sign of its increasing importance. The members of this group were drawn from the gentry and had often received a professional training as lawyers or estate administrators. They were already prominent in local government, but under Edward they moved into positions of authority at the centre, and as the crown's power expanded so did theirs.

The names of more than 120 Councillors survive for Edward's reign, but they never all met at any one time. In practice the Council consisted of anything from nine to twelve members, and the maximum recorded attendance was twenty. The King summoned whom he liked when he liked, and although the Council would, if Edward so wished, discuss major issues and make recommendations, he accepted or rejected these as he saw fit [27; 28; 34].

While Edward's accession resulted in a sharp decline in the influence of the magnates on government, the new King was not anti-noble by temperament. As a magnate himself Edward felt at ease in the company of his fellow nobles and during the course of his reign he created over thirty peerages. A number of these new peers held important offices at Court – William Hastings for instance, who was made a baron in 1461, was Lord Chamberlain of the household for the whole of Edward's reign – but their principal function, like that of the old nobles, was to maintain order in the localities, and Edward deliberately built up aristocratic influence where he believed it was in his interest to do so. He presented Hastings with large grants of confiscated property in the Midlands; he gave William Herbert lands and offices to establish his predominance in Wales; and in the second part of his reign he made his brother, Richard, Duke of Gloucester, the greatest magnate in the north [28].

The maintenance of order continued to be a problem throughout Edward's reign, for the effects of the civil wars did not disappear overnight. Also, Edward made little attempt to curb retaining, which was a major source of disorder since it allowed his greater subjects to maintain what were, in effect, private armies. However, when disorder became a major threat to the security of his throne, Edward would act swiftly and decisively. During the first part of his reign in particular he made extensive use of the Constable's Court, or Court of Chivalry, which, under the ruthless leadership of John Tiptoft, Earl of Worcester and Constable of England, dealt in a summary fashion with those it deemed guilty of insurrection. Edward also issued frequent commissions of oyer and terminer, empowering the members to put down riots and other breaches of the peace. These commissions would usually include Councillors, household officials, nobles and judges, and their combined authority was calculated to overawe all but the most arrogant offenders [34]. However, Edward was not content to act solely by deputies. He was always on the move himself, travelling in state from one disturbed area to another and using the majesty of his kingly office, as well as his own abundant energy and self-confidence, to impose order. In some instances – particularly when his own adherents were themselves the cause of unrest – Edward preferred to turn a blind eye to what was going on, but in general he took a firm stand and demonstrated beyond any shadow of doubt his determination to be obeyed.

2 YORKIST FINANCIAL ADMINISTRATION

The weakness of royal government in the mid-fifteenth century had sprung, in large part, from shortage of money. The first Lancastrian had enjoyed a revenue of some £90,000 annually, but by the closing years of Henry VI's reign this had diminished to £24,000 [34]. Edward realised that in order to make the crown strong again he would have to restore it to solvency, but this turned out to be a slow process. He could have called on Parliament for assistance, but Parliament had become a focus for opposition to the monarch during the Lancastrian period and he may well have thought that a break with the past implied a reduction in its role. He summoned only six Parliaments during a reign of twenty-three years, and he assured members in 1467 that 'I purpose to live upon mine own, and not to charge my subjects but in great and urgent causes concerning the weal of themselves and also the defence of them and of this my realm, rather than my own pleasure'. Edward was as good as his word, for although he received nearly £190,000 in parliamentary taxation during the course of his reign, he used this to meet the 'extraordinary' costs of suppressing rebellions at home and waging war abroad.

As far as the 'ordinary' revenue was concerned, Edward was dependent upon his own resources. When he seized the crown he took over the royal estates, including those of the Duchy of Lancaster, and he also held extensive properties in his own right as Duke of York. Furthermore, he persuaded Parliament to pass four Acts of resumption which restored to the crown a good deal of the land given away by Henry VI. The mere possession of property, however, was no guarantee of wealth: the crown lands needed to be administered in such a way that they would yield a substantial and increasing profit. The medieval monarchy had developed, in the Exchequer, a sophisticated and elaborate mechanism for collecting and auditing the King's revenues, but its procedure was slow and during the civil wars it had fallen badly behind. Edward wanted to exercise the same close, personal control over his revenues as he did over policy-making, and for this reason he increasingly by-passed the Exchequer and made the royal Chamber – which had hitherto dealt only with the finances of the Court and household – into a national treasury.

From early in his reign Edward began the practice of removing lands from Exchequer control and placing them instead under specially appointed receivers and surveyors who accounted to the Chamber. Sir Thomas Vaughan, the Treasurer of the Chamber, thereby became a key figure in the administration of the royal finances, but Edward himself took an active role, inspecting the Chamber accounts and giving Vaughan instructions by word of mouth. 'By 1483', in the words of Edward's biographer, 'there had emerged a system of highly personal financial control, centred on the Chamber, which anticipated in all essentials the structure once thought to have been created by the early Tudors' [34 *p. 375*].

Edward had other sources of revenue apart from the crown lands. In 1465 Parliament voted him Customs duties (tonnage and poundage) for life, and as foreign trade expanded with the return of more settled conditions the Customs became increasingly valuable. By the end of the reign they were bringing in some £34,000 a year, which was considerably more than the net yield of the royal estates. Edward also made substantial profits through engaging in trading ventures on his own account. The crown's feudal rights, especially wardship, were a further source of income, but Edward had to tread carefully here since he risked provoking a hostile reaction from the landowners. Following the conclusion of peace with France by the Treaty of Picquigny in 1475 (see below, p. 81), Edward added a pension of £10,000 to his annual revenues. The result of all these developments was that by 1475 Edward was solvent – the first English sovereign to be in this happy state for more than a century – and by the time he died he had pushed the crown's income up to some £70,000 a year. This was not as high as under Henry IV, but nearly three times what it had been at the time of Edward's accession [34].

PART TWO: ANALYSIS

1   THE NEW KING

Yorkist rule came to an abrupt end in August 1485 when Henry Tudor defeated and killed Edward IV's brother and successor, Richard III. The new King, Henry VII, was the posthumous son of Edmund Tudor, who had been created Earl of Richmond by his half-brother, Henry VI. Edmund's mother was Catherine of France, who had first been married to Henry V and, after his death, took as her second husband one of her household officers, Owen Tudor, who belonged to an old Welsh family. However, Henry's real claim to the throne came from his mother, Margaret Beaufort, who was descended from Edward III through the marriage of his fourth (but third surviving) son, John of Gaunt, Duke of Lancaster, to Catherine Swynford (see Genealogy, p. 115). But Catherine's children had been born before she married Gaunt, and although an Act of Richard II's reign removed the stain of illegitimacy from the Beauforts, Henry IV subsequently inserted a clause excluding them from any right of succession to the crown.

Henry was born in January 1457 at Pembroke Castle and was brought up by his uncle Jasper Tudor, Earl of Pembroke. However, after the defeat and subsequent murder of Henry VI in 1471 it seemed safer for Henry Tudor, who was now head of the house of Lancaster, to move out of the Yorkists' range. He and Jasper therefore fled to Brittany. Henry spent fourteen years in exile, waiting for an opportunity to return and claim what he regarded as his inheritance. In the autumn of 1483 the moment seemed to have arrived, for Henry planned a landing in England to coincide with the Duke of Buckingham's rebellion against Richard III. But the rebellion broke out prematurely, Buckingham was captured and executed, and although Henry set sail, his ships were dispersed in a storm. When he arrived off the English coast he decided not to land, perhaps because a call to arms issued by the Bishop of Exeter a day after Buckingham's execution attracted only limited support [37].

The triumphant Richard now put pressure on the Duke of

Brittany to hand over the troublesome exile, and Henry had to take refuge in France, where, in November 1484, he began to style himself King – the first time a pretender to the English throne had ever dared to assume the royal title before he had actually laid hands on the crown [40]. Henry may have hoped thereby to win support from those Yorkists who had never forgiven Richard for murdering Edward IV's young sons, Edward V and Richard, Duke of York – 'the Princes in the Tower' – in order to seize the throne for himself. If so, it may be significant that Sir John Risley, a former servant of Edward IV, chose this moment to defect to Henry, along with his sons and a handful of retainers [64].

There was little chance that Henry's small forces, even with the addition of Yorkist malcontents, would succeed in toppling Richard. But Charles VIII of France offered money, a fleet, and an army of 4,000 mercenaries, gambling that Henry, if ever he became King, would pursue pro-French policies. With this invaluable support, Henry set out for England once again, and on 7 August 1485 landed in Milford Haven, thereby outflanking Richard's southern defences, and marched swiftly through Wales and the West Midlands, leaving Richard too little time to gather his entire strength [36; 42; 93]. Though a trickle of volunteers came in to join the pretender, there was no general rising in his favour. But if Henry's cause aroused little enthusiasm, neither did Richard's. Only nine nobles, less than a quarter of the English baronage, joined the King at Bosworth, in Leicestershire, where the two armies met on 22 August, and not all of these were firmly committed to him [27]. Henry had good reason to hope that when the moment of decision came, some of them would hold back or even switch their allegiance. A key figure in his calculations was Thomas, Lord Stanley, who had become the third husband of Lady Margaret Beaufort and was therefore Henry's stepfather. Stanley deliberately avoided committing his forces to the battle. So at first did his brother, Sir William Stanley. But at the crucial moment, when Henry was losing ground, Sir William sent his 3,000 men to attack Richard in the rear. Richard knew the game was up. With a cry of 'Treachery!' he plunged into the heart of the battle and was struck down. The circlet of gold which adorned his brow fell off and was picked up by Lord Stanley, who placed it on Henry's head. Richard's naked body was slung over a horse and carried ignominiously away to Leicester, where it was buried [10].

Henry VII, who was now, at the age of twenty-eight, King of England, was a virtual stranger to his kingdom, having spent the first part of his life in Wales and the rest in exile. He was slim, taller than average, and his face, with its straight, Roman nose, its pronounced cheekbones, and its large hooded eyes, was one of considerable nobility [*Doc. 1*]. We are accustomed to think of Henry as a silent, grave man, whose countenance, as Bacon said, 'was reverend, and a little like a churchman', but this is only part of the picture. It is true that he cultivated discretion to such a point that men could never be certain what he was thinking, but despite Bacon's comment that where Henry's pleasures were concerned 'there is no news of them', the new King had his lighter side. Apart from hunting and hawking, to which he was devoted, he enjoyed gambling and playing tennis. When the old royal palace of Sheen, in Surrey, was destroyed by fire, he replaced it with a new one which he named in honour of his Yorkshire earldom of Richmond – though his subjects called it Rich Mount because of the large amount of money (over £20,000) spent on its construction and furnishings. It included not only 'pleasant dancing chambers' but also 'houses of pleasure to disport in, at chess, tables, dice [and] cards', as well as 'butts for archers, and goodly tennis plays' [68 *p. 25*]. Richmond Palace covered ten acres and was surmounted by a cluster of onion-shaped domes, each with its gilded weather-vane decorated with the royal arms. Virtually nothing remains of it today, and the same is true of the medieval palace of Placentia, overlooking the Thames at Greenwich, which Henry remodelled. His work was swept away in the late seventeenth century by the creation of the royal hospital which now occupies the site. Yet some idea of the richness and quality of Henry's creations is to be gained from two of his achievements which have survived: the chapel of King's College, Cambridge, which he brought to completion, and the jewel-like Henry VII Chapel at Westminster Abbey, where he is buried.

Although Henry made provision for his courtiers' entertainment, in general he maintained a high degree of formality and consciously cultivated 'magnificence', taking as his model the Dukes of Burgundy, whose court was regarded as the finest in Christendom. 'Magnificence' implied not simply rich costumes and elaborate ceremonial but also the encouragement of artists and men of letters. Edward IV had purchased books and tapestries in an unsystematic manner, but Henry became an avid and discerning collector of both. He was not content to leave his books in the custody of the Wardrobe, as Edward had done, but established the royal library as a separate department of the household, with a Keeper to look after it. Its principal holdings consisted of histories, romances and verse epics, written mainly in French, as well as illuminated manuscripts. Indeed, it was the existence of the royal library that led to the setting up of a school of Flemish illustrators at the English Court. Among the poets patronised by Henry were John Skelton, whom he appointed tutor to his son and namesake, and Bernard André, the blind poet from Toulouse, whom he chose as the official Court chronicler. In the words of one historian, 'no previous English King had been so acutely aware of the political advantages of surrounding himself with literary servants' whose main task was 'to present Tudor policy in as forceful and impressive a manner as possible' [41 *p. 132*].

Henry's admiration for Burgundy did not mean that he was impervious to Renaissance influences. He appointed the Italian poet, Peter Carmelianus, to the newly created post of Latin secretary, and he commissioned another Italian, Polydore Vergil, to write a history of England. These men were humanists, in the sense that their learning was firmly rooted in the classics, particularly Latin, but because they came at this early stage in the reception of the Renaissance in England they were later overshadowed by greater figures. Much the same is true of Henry's cultural achievement as a whole, for his commitment to Burgundian values, so natural at the time, seemed old-fashioned and even obscurantist to the next generation of humanists. Yet he 'transformed the royal household into a major influence upon the development of the fine arts in England. By the same means, he set a standard of courtly patronage and established a distinctive royal style for his descendants' [41 *p. 164*].

4 THE ROYAL FINANCES

EXCHEQUER AND CHAMBER

The system of Chamber finance which the Yorkists had developed could only work satisfactorily if the King actively supervised it. Henry VII, however, had no experience in financial administration, and he was in any case fully occupied with securing his hold upon his newly won throne. The collection and auditing of the crown's revenues might have broken down altogether had not the Exchequer resumed its earlier and traditional role as guardian of the royal finances. But it had not been designed to deal with the complexities of fifteenth-century estate administration and had neither the personnel nor the techniques to cope with the task confronting it. As a consequence, the crown's income from land declined from about £25,000 per annum at the end of Richard III's reign to just £11,700 in the first year of Henry's. Furthermore, it soon became apparent that the Exchequer's methods in raising and disbursing revenue were not always well suited to the needs of the crown. The Exchequer customarily operated through a system known as assignment: revenues raised by individual royal collectors were centrally 'assigned' to designated recipients, who were frequently paid locally by the collectors themselves rather than by the Exchequer at Westminster. This system largely avoided the need to transport coin, which was expensive, but it had the effect of preventing the Exchequer from building up its stock of ready cash. Indeed, between 1460 and 1485 only 28 per cent of the funds handled by the Exchequer took the form of money. Lack of cash meant that the Exchequer often had to borrow in order to meet the running costs of government. More importantly, it meant that the Exchequer was generally ill-prepared to meet the crown's needs quickly, particularly in an emergency. In 1490 Henry VII was forced to intervene personally after the Exchequer told the Clerk of the Council, Thomas Rydon, that he would not be able to go to Spain on an important diplomatic mission, as the King had ordered, since there was no money available. Two years later the Exchequer was unable to find the £40 needed to pay the arrears of another emissary, and was obliged to borrow the money from a London alderman [47].

Perhaps the principal disadvantage of the Exchequer system was that it denied the King complete control over his own finances. This presumably explains why the Exchequer's reassertion of its dominant role was short-lived. Henry quickly came to see the advantages of the alternative Chamber system, which would enable him to reward his servants or officials on the spot from cash reserves under his direct control, decide the order in which he wished to pay his expenses, keep a watchful eye on outgoings, and monitor his accounts with a reasonable degree of accuracy. Crucially, it would also enable him to lay his hands on ready money in an emergency, and this was a vital factor in explaining his political survival. In Dr Starkey's words, 'The Tudors had a quick way with rebellion and it depended more on the gold in their coffers than on the overrated quality of their propagandists' [53 *p. 203*].

The Tudor revival of Chamber finance began shortly after the Battle of Stoke in 1487, when Henry VII was no longer so preoccupied with threats to his security. Estate revenues were withdrawn from the Exchequer's control and placed in the hands of the Chamber, whose treasurer became the *de facto* receiver-general of crown lands. So, too, were the profits of justice, feudal dues and, from 1492, the French pension (see below, p. 81). Nevertheless, for reasons which remain unclear, the transition was effected only slowly, and it was not until the mid-1490s that the Chamber began to eclipse the Exchequer. By the end of Henry's reign its predominance was assured, for it was handling some 90 per cent of the crown's income. Yet, though the Exchequer had been overshadowed, it continued to function, for unlike the Chamber its existence as a separate revenue department was enshrined in statute, while for administrative reasons it retained control over Customs' receipts and sheriffs' accounts. Its judicial functions in matters such as the pursuit of debtors also remained vital.

It has recently been argued by Professor Alsop that the re-emergence of the Chamber as the dominant revenue department was not due to any shortcomings in the Exchequer. Far from being a moribund institution, he argues, the Exchequer was always looking for ways in which to improve its procedures. For instance, by 1505 it had devised a new type of document, known as 'the declaration of the state of the treasury', which arranged revenue and expenditure by kind rather than chronologically, as had hitherto been the case. Alsop furthermore denies that the Exchequer was unable to provide cash on demand, and he asserts that the reasons for the shift towards a Chamber system should be sought 'in the political and administrative conditions of the age' and in the personality of the new monarch [43 *pp. 179–99*]. However, while the new Chamber system undoubtedly suited Henry VII's temperament, this does not imply that Alsop's re-interpretation is necessarily correct. On the contrary, the vigour which he attributes to the Exchequer may have been in large part a response to its declining role as a treasury. And as for Alsop's claim that the Exchequer could always lay its hands on sufficient cash to meet royal demands, this has been effectively demolished by Professor Currin [47].

One of the disadvantages of using the Chamber as a national treasury was that it did not possess the elaborate auditing machinery which the Exchequer had developed over the course of its long history. Edward IV had appointed *ad hoc* auditors to examine those accounts which were no longer to be submitted to Exchequer scrutiny, and for some time Henry continued this practice, while acting himself as his own chief auditor. The head of the Chamber was its Treasurer, a post held from 1492 onwards by John Heron. He presented his accounts regularly to the King, who inspected them carefully and, until April 1503, signified his approval by initialling each entry. Deteriorating eyesight forced Henry thereafter to limit his efforts to the initialling of each page. Without this close personal supervision the system of Chamber finance could never have worked as well as it did, but Henry came increasingly to rely upon the advice and assistance of Sir Reginald Bray, who was one of his few close friends. Bray had learnt the business of estate management as surveyor and receiver-general to Sir Henry Stafford, and he entered royal service as a consequence of Stafford's marriage to the widowed Lady Margaret Beaufort, mother of Henry VII. After Henry became King he appointed Bray Chancellor of the Duchy of Lancaster, thereby making him responsible for administering one of the greatest landed estates in the kingdom. Duchy procedures had become somewhat lethargic, but Bray breathed new life into them by appointing special commissioners to enquire into cases of neglect or delay. This confirmed Henry's high opinion of him, and he became the King's principal adviser on financial matters [44]. In February 1486 Henry even appointed him Lord Treasurer, a position normally reserved for a member of the nobility, although

Bray surrendered the office to Lord Dinham less than five months later [58].

It was Bray, therefore, who assumed the responsibility for developing new auditing machinery for the Chamber, in collaboration with Heron and other household officials. They instituted the practice of holding regular meetings at which the Chamber accounts were submitted to intensive scrutiny. After Bray's death in 1503, his place was taken by Sir Robert Southwell, who was assisted by the Bishop of Carlisle and a dozen or so other officials, most of them members either of the royal Council or the Prince of Wales's household. As early as the mid-1490s this committee of auditors was being referred to as the 'General Surveyors', but in fact a formally constituted Court of General Surveyors did not come into existence until Henry VIII's reign. Nevertheless, Southwell and his associates functioned as an informal court of audit, developing routines for examining local receivers and going through their accounts before submitting them to the King [48].

The transformation of the Chamber from a household department into a national treasury was accompanied by a further development: the emergence of a Secret or Privy Chamber, whose chief officer – indeed, for some time its only one – was the Groom of the Stool. He acted independently of the Treasurer of the Chamber and became, in effect, the keeper of the King's privy purse, paying out 'rewards' on Henry's behalf and making whatever purchases the King needed for his private use [69]. The reasons for the emergence of the Privy Chamber remain unclear, but it may have been a response to the discovery in 1494 of the treason of the Lord Chamberlain of the household, Sir William Stanley (see below, pp. 32–3).

LAND AS A SOURCE OF REVENUE

The Chamber derived the bulk of its revenue from the royal lands. Henry VII held more property than any sovereign since the Norman Conquest. This was partly due to good fortune, but it was also the result of Henry's ruthless disregard for the property rights of his subjects. The core of the royal estate was formed by the duchies of Lancaster and Cornwall and the earldoms of Richmond and Chester, which from about 1487 onwards were withdrawn from Exchequer control. To this core of properties, Henry added the bulk of the Duchy of York, following his marriage to Edward IV's eldest daughter, Elizabeth of York. The only portion of the Yorkist inheritance which was denied to Henry – as to Edward IV and Richard III – was that which belonged to Edward IV's mother, Cecily, Duchess of York. However, when she died in 1495 her property passed to Henry.

The King's propensity to ride roughshod over the legal rights of his subjects was not prompted solely by greed. Admittedly, the bargain struck between Henry and the elderly and childless Earl of Nottingham in 1489 – whereby Nottingham disinherited his brother in favour of the King, in return for his own elevation to the rank of Marquess – gave Henry eventual possession of one of the richest baronies in England, but at the same time it reduced the threat from a magnate family that might have become overmighty. The same mixture of motives applies to Henry's treatment of Anne Beauchamp, widow of Richard, Earl of Warwick, 'the Kingmaker' (d. 1471). In 1487 Anne had her substantial share of the Warwick estates restored to her by Act of Parliament, but almost immediately – and presumably by prior arrangement – she settled the bulk of these on the crown, thereby disinheriting her grandson, Edward, Earl of Warwick, whom Henry held close prisoner in the Tower of London [93].

While always eager to acquire more land, Henry nevertheless resisted the urge to assert his right to all the property which had earlier belonged to the crown. Although two Acts of resumption were passed, in 1485 and 1487, giving him the nominal ownership of lands held by the crown in October 1455, the principal purpose of these was not to dispossess the existing occupiers, which would have been politically counter-productive, but to ensure that in the many instances when ownership was uncertain and disputed the crown would be well placed to assert its claims.

Constant additions were made to the royal estate throughout the reign by the use of Acts of attainder against the King's enemies [*Doc. 15*]. Just under 140 individuals suffered in this way, and although one-third of the attainders were reversed, the net effect was a considerable transfer of property to the crown [20; 27]. Among Henry's greatest gains was the estate of his Chamberlain, Sir William Stanley, which brought in £9,000 in cash and an income of £1,000 a year. Other property forfeited to the crown included the lands of the Duke of Norfolk, who was killed fighting for Richard III at Bosworth, though some of these were subsequently returned to Norfolk's son, the Earl of Surrey.

Henry was careful to alienate very few of the lands he acquired.

The main recipients of his grants were his mother, Lady Margaret Beaufort, and his uncle, Jasper Tudor, whom he created Duke of Bedford. In the case of his mother, who received manors and lordships valued at £3,394 per annum, Henry could feel confident that the property bestowed on her would revert to the crown at her death. It was less certain that the same would happen to the vast estate conferred on Bedford in South Wales, but as luck would have it Bedford died childless in 1495, and Henry was able to use this inheritance to endow his second son, Prince Henry.

FEUDAL AND PREROGATIVE REVENUE

As well as the income he derived direct from the royal lands, Henry also profited from the crown's prerogative rights. There were two main aspects to this prerogative. In the first place the King, as the greatest of all feudal lords, could claim the rights which belonged, by ancient custom, to any lord. Should he be unfortunate enough to be captured and held to ransom he could demand an aid to raise the necessary sum. He could also call for aids on the occasion of the marriage of his eldest daughter and the knighting of his eldest son. Feudal aids could not be levied without the consent of the tenants-in-chief (which meant, in practice, Parliament), but no consent was needed for the feudal incidents, of which the most important was wardship. If a tenant-in-chief died leaving an under-age heir, the boy became a ward of the King and his estates passed under royal guardianship, to compensate the King for the loss of military service implicit in the succession of a minor. In practice, the King usually sold the wardship to the highest bidder [*Doc. 2*], and there was no shortage of takers since the man who acquired the guardianship of a ward usually assumed control of the boy's estates as well. The guardian was forbidden by law to despoil the estates for which he was responsible, but 'despoiling' was an ill-defined term and the high price paid for wardships suggests that those who bought them calculated on making a substantial profit. Wardship did not necessarily involve the intervention of a third party, however. A mother or other relative could apply for the guardianship of the minor, and the request might well be granted – but only, of course, upon payment.

Although wardship was the most lucrative of the feudal incidents to which the King was entitled, it was not the only one. When a ward came of age he had to pay a due called 'livery' before he could assume control of his inheritance. If the heir was a woman, she needed the King's permission to marry, and this was also a source of profit. The King would either sell the right to marry the heiress to the highest bidder or, if she was rich enough, accept a substantial sum in return for leaving her free to make her own choice. If there was no heir to an estate, the King would exercise the right of escheat and take the lands back into his own hands. He could also exercise this right if a tenant-in-chief was found to be a lunatic or an idiot. The theory behind all these incidents dated from the early medieval period, when the military organisation of the country really did depend upon the knight-service of tenants-in-chief. By the time Henry seized the throne, indentured retainers and commissions of array (see below, p. 40) had replaced feudal obligations as the most effective way of raising an army, but feudalism, although deprived of its *raison d'être*, remained in existence as a financial system [*Doc. 2*].

From early in his reign Henry appointed commissioners to investigate the extent of his feudal rights. Laboriously but inexorably they pursued their enquiries, ferreting out under-age heirs whose existence had been concealed in an attempt to evade wardship. The last fifty 'Inquisitions Post-Mortem' for Henry's reign record the discovery of twenty-eight under-age heirs [5]. The average lifespan was short in early Tudor England: hence the frequency of inheritance by minors, and the significance of wardship. Where the tenure by which an estate was held was disputed or uncertain, the commissioners would invariably rule in favour of the crown, but landowners had a right of appeal to the common-law courts. In 1505, for example, a royal commission in Northumberland decreed that twenty tenancies of the Earl of Northumberland belonged rightly to the crown, but King's Bench, on an appeal by the tenants, reversed most of these verdicts [44; 50].

As a result of Henry's remorseless pressure, his income from wardship rose substantially. In 1487 he obtained less than £300 from this source, but by 1494 receipts were running at over £1,500 and by 1507 they had soared to more than £6,000 a year. At first Henry appointed household officers *ad hoc* to deal with wardship, but as the revenue increased the need for specialisation became apparent. This was particularly the case after the death of Bray in 1503, and it was no coincidence that the same year saw the creation of the office of Master of Wards, with the responsibility for 'overseeing, managing and selling the wardships of all lands which may be in the King's hands'. Sir John Hussey, the first Master, quickly built up an organisation, and by 1509 there were probably local masters, receivers-general and auditors in every county, all responsible to Hussey, who was, of course, responsible to the King [51].

In addition to his feudal prerogative the King had privileges which belonged to him as monarch. As guardian of his subjects he had the right – indeed, the duty – to make them live in peace and good order, to punish those who resisted, to take bonds of good behaviour, and to supplement the course of the common law where it was deficient. All aspects of the prerogative, feudal and non-feudal alike, had this in common, that they were potential sources of profit, and the responsibility for enforcing prerogative rights was therefore assumed by Bray and his associates in the informal court of audit [48]. After Bray's death, however, there was no one specifically responsible for enforcing prerogative rights other than wardship. Henry filled this gap, in August 1508, by creating a new office of Surveyor of the King's Prerogative and appointing Sir Edward Belknap to it [50]. Belknap had a mixed bag of duties. One of his principal tasks was to search out and fine widows of tenants-in-chief who had remarried without first obtaining leave from the King. He was also required to improve the effectiveness of common-law procedures by seizing the lands of all those who had been convicted of felonies or murder or had been outlawed for failing to comply with the orders of the courts. In addition, the King instructed Belknap to collect debts that were owing to the crown, as well as fines which the King himself frequently assessed for breaches of the law. Much of this activity overlapped with that of the Council Learned (see below, p. 29), and Belknap in fact worked hand in hand with Empson and Dudley. It was this association with men who came to be identified with the more extortionate aspects of Henry VII's rule that led to the winding-up of the office of Surveyor of the King's Prerogative early in Henry VIII's reign.

PARLIAMENTARY GRANTS, LOANS, AND BENEVOLENCES

Henry's first Parliament, which met in 1485, made him a life grant of tonnage (on imported wine) and poundage (mainly on exported wool). The grant, as was customary, was made 'in especial for the safeguard and keeping of the sea', but in practice there was no restriction on the King's use of it. The yield of tonnage and poundage increased as trade flourished, and Henry's success in restoring ordered conditions and promoting commerce was directly rewarded by a larger income from this source.

In spite of the grant of tonnage and poundage, Henry was short of money in the early years of his reign. He had contracted debts as an exile which had to be repaid, he was forced to spend heavily on defending his throne against rival claimants, and his income from land dropped dramatically as a result of the temporary abandonment of Chamber finance (see above, p. 11). In 1486 and 1489 he sent commissioners into the counties to demand loans, averaging £1 a head, from his richer subjects [*Doc. 3*]. However crude a method of raising money, the forced loans seem to have aroused little or no protest. In fact, Henry's reputation was enhanced, and his creditworthiness improved, by the fact that the loans were apparently all repaid.

Henry, like Edward IV before him, aimed to 'live of his own' and not to trouble his subjects except in case of necessity. Such a necessity arose in 1487, with Simnel's rising (see below, pp. 75–6), and the Parliament which Henry summoned duly voted two Fifteenths and Tenths. This traditional tax theoretically provided one-fifteenth of the value of moveable goods of adult males in rural areas and one-tenth from those inhabiting towns and royal lands [*Doc. 4*]. In practice, however, the Fifteenth and Tenth had ossified into a fixed tax of some £29,000, which fell most heavily on the poorer sections of society. While this suited richer taxpayers, it was a source of frustration to the crown. Beginning in 1404, the Exchequer had made a number of experiments designed to relate taxation more closely to the actual distribution of wealth, but these had all failed. Henry VII renewed the attempt in 1489 when Parliament, which shared his determination to stop the French from absorbing Brittany (see below, pp. 76–81), voted him a nominal £100,000. Henry proposed that three-quarters of this sum should be raised from the laity through an income tax of 10 per cent and a levy on personal property, to be assessed by royal commissioners sent into the counties expressly for this purpose.

Parliament, which was concerned not to establish a potentially dangerous precedent, insisted that no records of individual wealth should be returned into the Exchequer. Nevertheless, the novelty of the tax caused widespread resentment and it only raised about £27,000: Parliament had to vote a conventional Fifteenth and Tenth to reduce the shortfall. In April 1489 an angry mob which had come together at Topcliffe, near Thirsk, in Yorkshire, murdered the King's tax collector, the Earl of Northumberland, so sparking off an uprising. Taxation was undoubtedly a major cause of the insurrection, though the only known rebel manifesto makes no mention of it, but concentrates on the King's attempts to limit the right of sanctuary (see below, p. 63). Yorkshiremen had a particular cause of grievance, since in 1474 Richard, Duke of Gloucester (future Richard III), who had his headquarters in the county, had persuaded his brother, Edward IV, to exempt its inhabitants from taxation in return for the monies they had laid out for the war against the Scots. This exemption had been abruptly terminated in 1487, when Yorkshire was required to contribute to the two Fifteenths and Tenths voted that year. Moreover, it seems that outstanding contributions were still being collected in the spring of 1489, when the demand came for further taxation [82].

The King's response to the murder of Northumberland and the rebels' siege of York was to raise an army to restore order. This he accomplished successfully, but he may have come to the conclusion that taxation levied at such a cost was self-defeating. If so, it would explain why, in May 1491, when Anne of Brittany called on him for support against France, the King chose to demand a 'Benevolence' from his richer subjects and corporations, and subsequently obtained a conventional grant of two Fifteenths and Tenths from Parliament [*Docs 4; 5*]. A Benevolence – so called because it was supposedly granted out of the *benevolentia* or goodwill of the giver – was regarded as a gift, not to be repaid. The main attraction of it from the King's point of view was the speed with which it could be collected, if all went well. There was also the advantage that since it did not affect the poorer elements in society it was unlikely to provoke resistance. However, though the 1491 Benevolence did not apparently cause a public outcry, it proved difficult to collect, and in 1495 parliamentary authority had to be obtained to secure payment of arrears. Even so, Sir John Heron's notebook reveals that as late as 1505 there were still unpaid contributions in 'every shire in England'.

The failure of the Benevolence may help explain why Henry chose to experiment once again with the tax system when a new foreign-policy crisis arose. Following the abortive Scottish invasion of the north in September 1496 (see below, p. 88), Henry summoned Parliament, which voted him two Fifteenths and Tenths as well as a further 'aid and subsidy'. Fiscal innovation led once more to rebellion, this time in the west country (see below, p. 43). Many of the rebels were poor, and could not understand why they should be called upon to pay for war in the opposite end of the kingdom, especially since the new subsidies were far more oppressive than the conventional Fifteenths and Tenths. Another factor which may have prompted the west country to revolt was the sheer size of the sums demanded: in 1497 the King levied £88,606 in taxation – the largest sum raised in any year of his entire reign. Henry made only one more demand for direct taxation after this date. In 1504, presumably because he was under pressure to raise money to keep the Emperor Maximilian and Philip of Burgundy from providing the renegade Earl of Suffolk with military support (see below, pp. 84–5), he asked Parliament to authorise the payment of two feudal aids, one for the knighting of his eldest son, the other for the marriage of his eldest daughter. The legality of such demands could not be contested, even though Prince Arthur had been knighted fifteen years before and was now dead, while the marriage of Princess Margaret to the King of Scotland had taken place in the previous year. However, members of Parliament feared that the demand for feudal aids was merely the pretext for an investigation into the nature of landholding throughout the kingdom, which might well increase their liability to wardship and other hated feudal incidents. Indeed, it seems that this was Henry's intention. Hence his anger when young Thomas More persuaded the Commons to reject his request (see below, p. 56). The Commons preferred, in the end, to offer a subsidy of £40,000, of which the King was graciously pleased to remit a quarter.

Apart from this incident in 1504, Henry had little trouble with Parliament where money was concerned. In fact, he raised nearly £282,000 through parliamentary taxation, which is equivalent to £11,750 per annum. In addition, he benefited from the taxes voted by the clergy in Convocation, which, if Professor Scarisbrick's estimate is correct for Henry VII's reign, were worth £9,000 a year [52]. All in all, then, it seems that Henry's subjects, lay and clerical, were contributing over £20,000 a year by way of taxation to the royal revenues.

HENRY'S FINANCIAL ACHIEVEMENT

Because of the complexities of Tudor accounting systems and the loss of many of the Chamber's financial records, it is not possible to give exact figures for Henry's finances. However, it has been estimated that the income from royal lands and wardship went up during his reign by 45 per cent, from an annual average of £29,000 to £42,000, while the Customs revenue rose from £33,000 to £40,000, an increase of 20 per cent. By the end of the reign the Chamber was handling well over £90,000 a year, excluding receipts from taxation, while another £12,500 passed through the Exchequer. If a further £10,000 is added for miscellaneous sources of revenue – and this figure may well be conservative, in view of the fact that payments from newly appointed bishops amounted to some £3,500 a year, while the sale of pardons for murder and other felonies yielded just under £4,000 in 1504–5 – then Henry's ordinary revenue amounted to about £113,000 per annum. When parliamentary and clerical taxation is added in, his total revenue works out at £133,000. The fact that this was some three times what Henry VI had been receiving in the mid-1430s is an indication of the success of the Yorkists and the first Tudor in restoring the crown's finances. It was even greater than the income enjoyed by the last of the pre-Lancastrian kings, Richard II, who was probably in receipt of £120,000 per annum, though it fell some way short of the revenue of £160,000 received by Richard's grandfather, Edward III. In other words, the Yorkist and early Tudor achievement consisted in restoring the finances of the crown to the relatively healthy state they had been in under the later Plantagenets.

The bare statistics of monies received do not give a complete picture of the financial situation. Certain revenues – varying in amount from the thousands of pounds paid annually to the Treasurer of Calais by the Company of the Staple to the small sums which sheriffs and other royal officials were allowed to deduct from their receipts for salaries and expenses – never passed through the central receiving agencies. The King also had a 'concealed income', for when he rewarded one of his servants by granting him a lucrative office or selling him a wardship at a nominal price he was saving himself money, and this was, in effect, a form of income. But even when generous allowance has been made for all these indirect sources of profit to the crown, it is unlikely that Henry VII's total revenue came anywhere near the £1,100,000 enjoyed by the Emperor or even the £800,000 which the King of France could expect every year.

By about 1490 Henry was solvent, and thereafter he enjoyed, in Bacon's phrase, 'the felicity of full coffers'. It was rumoured that he left a substantial fortune for his heir to squander, but in fact the Chamber contained only £9,000 at the time of his death. There may have been other, unrecorded sums in the hands of the Groom of the Stool, as well as the plate and jewels in which Henry had invested many thousands of pounds, but even when these are taken into account they do not add up to a 'fortune'. The perception that Henry had amassed an impressive hoard of coin may owe something to the Chamber system of finance, which brought large quantities of cash into his central Treasury. By comparison, few people remarked on the wealth of the French King, Louis XII, even though he was much richer than Henry, since little of his income came to him in the form of cash. As one historian has observed, 'Louis was rich on paper, and that impresses historians; Henry was rich in cash, and that impressed contemporaries' [*53 p. 203*]. Recognition of Henry VII's undoubted and major achievement in restoring the royal finances must not, therefore, obscure the fundamental truth that by European standards the English monarchy was under-endowed, circumscribed in its freedom of action, and dependent upon a considerable degree of co-operation, however grudgingly given, from those who were subject to it.

5 CENTRAL GOVERNMENT

THE COUNCIL

Henry VII's Council, in its composition and range of activities, was virtually identical to that of his immediate predecessors. Indeed, twenty-nine of his Councillors had held the same office under one or both of the Yorkist kings [20]. The largest group within the Council consisted of clerics, and among Henry's most trusted advisers was John Morton, whom he appointed Archbishop of Canterbury in 1486 and Lord Chancellor the following year. Morton had been closely involved in Buckingham's rebellion against Richard III, and he subsequently fled to join Henry in exile. He was a man of outstanding ability, played a major part in government, and continued to enjoy Henry's confidence down to the time of his death in 1500. Another former exile who became a prominent figure on the Council was Richard Fox, whom Henry chose to be his Secretary. In 1487 Fox was given the Bishopric of Exeter as well as the office of Lord Keeper of the Privy Seal, and Henry made frequent use of him on diplomatic missions.

The nobles were also represented on the Council, and there was no sign under Henry VII, any more than there had been under Edward IV, of a conscious policy to oust them from government. Ability and loyalty were the essential qualities so far as Henry was concerned, and his Council therefore included bearers of old titles, such as the Earls of Ormond, Oxford, and Surrey. Oxford was the Lord Great Chamberlain, and in 1507 the Spanish ambassador informed his king that while Henry had 'no confidential advisers', Oxford, 'who is of his blood, is . . . more in his confidence than any other person' [6 p. 436]. Oxford's office is sometimes confused with that of the newly ennobled Daubeney, who was Lord Chamberlain of the royal household from 1495. As such, Daubeney enjoyed constant access to Henry, and this led the rulers of Burgundy and France to lavish pensions on him [68] [Doc. 18 (a)]. Two other close associates of the King were both descendants of noble families. One was Sir Charles Somerset, illegitimate son of the second Duke of Somerset who had been executed in 1464 for his adherence to the Lancastrian cause. Sir Charles, later known as Lord Herbert, served Henry in a number of naval and diplomatic missions, and took Daubeney's place as Lord Chamberlain in 1508. The other close associate was Robert, Lord Willoughby de Broke, who had joined Henry in exile and returned with him to fight at Bosworth. Willoughby was employed by Henry as both a military and naval commander, and in 1488 was appointed Lord Steward of the household – a post which he held until his death in 1502. He was succeeded by another great nobleman, George Talbot, fourth Earl of Shrewsbury.

Although members of the nobility and senior churchmen played an important role in counselling the King, the influence of these two groups was undoubtedly reduced as Henry chose increasingly to rely on lesser landowners and professional men, especially lawyers. This was a novel development, but it would be a mistake to assume that it signalled the rise of the 'middle class' in government. In their aspirations and assumptions, and often indeed in their family connections, the men selected by Henry to advise him were close to the landed aristocracy and formed part of the upper section of English society. There is some doubt about Bray's background: his father was a citizen of Worcester, where he may have practised medicine [58]. But of the remaining non-clerical 'core' members of the Council, Daubeney was descended from an ancient Norman family established in England since the Conquest, Sir Richard Guildford was the son of a Kentish knight, while Sir Thomas Lovell and Sir John Risley were the children of Norfolk landowners. Yet it was this group that Perkin Warbeck denounced as 'caitiffs and villains of low birth'.

Among Councillors who emerged later in the reign, Edmund Dudley was the grandson of a Lancastrian peer; Sir Edward Belknap's family traced its descent from one of William the Conqueror's companions in arms; while Sir Edward Poynings's father was a Kentish squire and his mother a Paston. Sir Richard Empson, like Bray, was unusual in coming from an urban background, being the son of a leading citizen of Towcester in Northamptonshire [66]. But Empson's father owned property in the surrounding countryside, and the same was probably true of Bray's. In effect, then, Henry's Councillors came from gentry families and made their way in the world through estate management or the law

– or both. This is hardly surprising, for Henry VII was the greatest landowner in England and needed men who were skilled in property management and conversant with the intricacies of land law. He also required men of tact, diplomacy and linguistic ability to smoothe his relations with foreign powers. Bray, who was said to be 'plain and rough of speech', was hardly suited to such a task, but Sir John Risley, who was an even more assiduous attender at Council meetings than Bray, was employed on numerous diplomatic missions, and acted as interpreter in 1492 at a meeting between Henry and the French ambassador [64].

Members of the Council who were most intimately connected with Henry were well placed to exploit their position for maximum profit. Reginald Bray became one of the richest laymen in England, and the sum of £500 which he contributed to the Benevolence of 1491 was exceeded only by Lady Margaret Beaufort, the King's mother. Between 1485 and his death in 1503, Bray spent more than £10,000 in buying lands, as well as funding massive building operations not only on his own properties but also at St George's Chapel, Windsor [58].

The names of around 225 Councillors have been recorded for Henry VII's reign, but although Henry's Council was considerably larger than its Lancastrian predecessors or late Tudor successors, it was rare for 30 members to assemble at any one time [57]. The remainder were scattered throughout the country and irregular in their attendance: indeed, more than 40 of them seem never to have attended a single Council meeting. Taking the Council as a whole, 27 per cent of its members were clerics, 22 per cent officials, 20 per cent courtiers, 19 per cent peers, and 12 per cent lawyers – though these categories are not mutually exclusive [20]. The two Chief Justices, of King's Bench and Common Pleas, were frequent attenders, as was the King himself.

The number of Councillors present at any meeting varied from four (the quorum) to an exceptional 65, with seven as the commonest. The key figures were, of course, the holders of major office, and the prestige of the Council was increased by the fact that Henry kept his ministers in power for long periods, thereby demonstrating his confidence in them. From 1487 until 1509 there were only two Lord Chancellors, who between them held office for over twenty years. Lord Dinham was Treasurer from 1486 until his death in 1501, and thereafter it was the Earl of Surrey, while Richard Fox occupied the post of Lord Keeper of the Privy Seal from 1487 until well into Henry VIII's reign [76].

Henry VII's Council began work soon after his accession, and by the summer of 1486 it was holding regular formal meetings during the law terms in the room known as the Star Chamber. Though the Council warrants of Henry's reign are lost, we know something of its activity from extracts copied in the late sixteenth and early seventeenth centuries. It was particularly concerned with problems of internal security, the defence of the realm, and foreign affairs, and it also helped monitor the royal finances [54]. There was real debate at its meetings, though the ultimate decision on whether and how to implement its recommendations belonged to the King alone. Matters of foreign policy were usually given initial consideration by a small group of Councillors before being discussed by the full body.

The Council also fulfilled a judicial function, as part of its brief was to maintain law and order, though litigants were not normally given a hearing until the day's other business had been completed [59; 60]. There were occasions when the Council, acting upon information received, would take the initiative and either issue an executive order or summon the persons involved to appear before it. In most instances, however, it acted like any other court and waited for a plaintiff to lodge a formal complaint. The records have survived of some 300 cases considered by Henry VII's Council, of which the majority were initiated by private suitors and were overtly concerned with rioting. Yet such a charge was often no more than a legal fiction. A statute of Edward III's reign had forbidden the Council to deal with matters involving freehold, but by asserting that a riot had taken place a plaintiff could bring his case within the Council's competence. The advantage of this, from the plaintiff's point of view, was that the Council consisted of the most important men in the kingdom. Even if it simply remitted his case for consideration by a common-law court, he would have succeeded in speeding up the judicial process [*Doc. 6*]. Henry may initially have hoped and expected that his Council would take the lead in imposing order upon a turbulent society, but the revival and extension of conciliar jurisdiction had the effect of swamping the hard-pressed Council with civil actions that could best have been dealt with elsewhere. This development complicated Henry's problems rather than resolving them.

Although the Council was the linchpin of English government, it did not concern itself with every aspect of administration. Fiscal policy, for instance, and the enforcement of prerogative rights, were handled informally by a group consisting of Bray, Lovell, Morton and Fox, in company with the King. After the deaths of Morton and

Bray, these responsibilities were shared between the Council Learned and the informal court of audit which supervised the Chamber accounts. The Council also left law enforcement largely in the hands of specialised tribunals. One of these was the court, established by statute in 1487, charged with putting down 'unlawful maintenances, giving of liveries, signs and tokens, and retainders ... embraceries of his [i.e. the King's] subjects, untrue demeanings of sheriffs in making of panels [of jurors] and other untrue returns ... taking of money by juries [and] great riots and unlawful assemblies' [*Doc. 7*]. Subsequent to Henry VII's reign, the statute was given the title 'Pro Camera Stellata' and was later held to be the origin of the Court of Star Chamber, but in fact the 1487 tribunal was quite distinct from the Council in Star Chamber [*Doc. 8*]. There was, however, some overlap in personnel. It consisted of the three principal members of the Council – namely, the Chancellor, Treasurer, and Keeper of the Privy Seal – as well as two other Councillors, one lay and one clerical, and the two Chief Justices.

The organisation of the Council was, in practice, very fluid. Small groups of Councillors might be working on different problems at different places, but this did not mean that they ceased to be members of the parent body. One of the major splits was between those who stayed behind at Westminster when the King went on progress, and those who accompanied him; but when the King returned, the Councillors attendant made their way once again to the Star Chamber, and the two groups never developed into separate institutions. Only in relatively few cases did specialisation lead to the emergence of what were, in effect, autonomous bodies. One such was formed by a group of lesser Councillors consisting of clerics trained in civil and canon law, as well as a number of common lawyers. It had originally been set up under Richard III as a regular tribunal for poor men's causes, for the cost of bringing an action at common law put such a remedy beyond the range of the poor. This 'Court of Requests' lapsed in 1485, but during the latter part of Henry VII's reign poor men's causes were once more given special consideration. The personnel of this tribunal probably fluctuated to some extent, and it never became totally detached from its parent body, the Council. Nevertheless, it was already, in embryo, the Court of Requests for Poor Men's Causes that was to maintain an independent existence from Henry VIII's reign onwards [9 *pp. 187–90*]. By contrast, a body which achieved full separation from the Council under Henry VII was the Council Learned.

THE COUNCIL LEARNED

The Council Learned was a small body, with a maximum of twelve members, though they never all met together. The great majority of members had a legal training and were therefore 'learned in law' – hence the name given to this council [67]. It had close connections with the Duchy of Lancaster, whose Chancellor acted as a kind of president, and its meetings usually took place in the Duchy Chamber. The Council Learned was in existence from at least 1495, though only a separate institution from 1499 onwards, and Bray, as Chancellor of the Duchy, played a prominent part in its proceedings. However, its reputation – or rather its notoriety – increased after Sir Richard Empson became Chancellor of the Duchy in 1504 [66]. Empson was a Northamptonshire lawyer who had lost his position as Attorney-General of the Duchy at the accession of Richard III, but regained it shortly after Bosworth. His close associate was Edmund Dudley [65], a former under-sheriff of London who was chosen as Speaker of the House of Commons in 1504 – a position which Empson had himself occupied in 1491. It should, however, be borne in mind that Empson and Dudley were friends and colleagues of Bray, and had presumably learnt many of their methods from him.

The Council Learned dealt with a wide range of prosecutions on behalf of the crown – for instance, the export of wool without paying Customs, the transference of land to a corporation without licence of mortmain, the failure to take up knighthood, the misconduct of sheriffs, and the infringement of the King's rights of wardship and livery [67]. It also acted as a debt-collecting agent, operating in this respect as the enforcement arm of the Chamber. The Council Learned had a great deal of discretion when it came to imposing penalties. Where these concerned penal statutes (see below, p. 59) the fine was often fixed by law. But infringements of the royal prerogative were a matter for the King's discretion, and the Council Learned could demand as much or as little as it thought appropriate. This was also the case with suitors seeking a favour from the King, such as hiring one of his ships or asking him not to enforce his rights of wardship or lunacy [*Doc. 10*].

The Council Learned was involved in the drawing up of bonds and recognisances, binding the persons concerned to good behaviour under threat of a financial penalty [*Doc. 14*]. One of the main advantages to the crown of using such instruments was that those who broke their recognisances did not have to be prosecuted at the common law, which could be a long process and of uncertain outcome. All the crown needed to do was to sue the offenders for debt on their bonds. Another advantage of these devices was that they spread the burden of law enforcement more widely, since responsibility for ensuring good conduct fell not only on the person bound, but also on his friends, neighbours or relatives, who were often required to act as suretors. The use of such instruments was not uncommon as a means of holding the aristocracy in check, for they had been widely employed since the reign of Henry V, but Henry VII extended their scope by imposing them on the greater part of the English aristocracy [27]. Out of 62 peerage families in existence during the reign of the first Tudor, 46 or 47 were for a time 'at the King's mercy', either through Acts of attainder, which Henry was much less willing to reverse than Edward IV had been, or, more commonly, through bonds and recognisances. However, few nobles were bound over for good behaviour before 1502, and one historian has concluded that 'the extensive use of recognisances by Henry VII in his dealings with many of his wealthier subjects, including most of the English peerage, was a characteristic feature of his rule only in the course of the last seven years of his reign' [93 *p. 66*]. One reason for this sharp increase in their use was Henry's fears for the succession, following the death of Prince Arthur in April 1502 and of Queen Elizabeth the following year. Growing royal avarice may also have played a part, though Dudley's account book for the period 1504–8 shows that only £30,000 of nearly £220,000 which he recorded as having 'collected' was actually paid. The rest consisted of promises to pay, and these recognisances were duly listed in the King's books, ready to be put into effect if the debtor misbehaved himself [20].

During the latter part of his reign, Henry effectively put the peerage on probation. The penalties he imposed for anti-social behaviour could be substantial: in 1504, to take one example, the fourth Earl of Northumberland and the Archbishop of York were both commanded to give bonds of £2,000 each to keep the peace towards each other. Some peers were required to enter into more than one recognisance, such as the unfortunate Lord Mountjoy, whose total of 23 was the highest number demanded of any nobleman during the reign. Even Henry's closest friends were not safe. The Earl of Shrewsbury, despite his record of devoted service, was required to give bonds totalling some £500 in his own behalf, and later on bound himself in respect of the good behaviour of some of his friends, with the result that by the end of the reign he was standing surety for five different groups of people and was 'endangered' for more than £5,000.

This method of preserving peace was clearly effective, but to the nobles who were its victims it probably seemed more like blackmail. There was little they could do about it while Henry lived, but they focused their resentment on Empson and Dudley, who were the King's principal agents, and on the Council Learned through which they operated. Empson and Dudley were undoubtedly ruthless in their enforcement of royal rights; they were accused, among other things, of falsely asserting that certain lands were held by feudal tenure and therefore subject to wardship and other incidents which were profitable to the King but vexatious to his subjects [*Doc. 11*]. They were also guilty from time to time of corrupt practices. Thomas Sunnyff was accused of murdering his (stillborn) child, and Dudley demanded payment of £500, saying 'Agree with the King, or else you must go to the Tower'. When Sunnyff refused he was imprisoned, and although he appealed to the common law, the judges were ordered by the King not to intervene. Sunnyff eventually paid up, for fear that he would otherwise rot in prison. Dudley later expressed remorse for his action but insisted that he had not made a single penny out of it. All the money went to Henry [102, I].

Dudley subsequently listed more than 80 cases in which he believed that Henry had acted extortionately by taking excessive bonds, and declared that it had been the King's express purpose 'to have many persons in his danger at his pleasure' [20, *p. 311*]. In the reaction that set in after Henry's death, nearly 200 recognisances were cancelled, and in a quarter of the cases it was specifically stated that this was because they had been unjustly extorted. Empson and Dudley were arrested in 1509 and charged with plotting the death of the new King, Henry VIII. They were subsequently attainted by Parliament and in August 1510 were beheaded on Tower Hill. William Smith, another of Henry VII's agents, who had been the Council Learned's enforcement officer in the north-west, was stripped of his offices and accused of promoting malicious prosecutions. Unlike his masters, however, he escaped death.

POLITICS AND THE COURT

Francis Bacon, who published his *History of the Reign of King Henry the Seventh* in 1622, described Henry's Court as devoid of politics and therefore free of dangerous factional intrigues. As late as

1987 this view was echoed by Professor Davies, who claimed that Henry 'avoided that strife of "factions" which so dominated the politics of the reigns of Edward IV and of Henry VIII' [39 *p.* 6]. More recently, however, Dr Gunn has reminded us that Bacon, who had just been dismissed from office as Lord Chancellor, was not writing an objective account of Henry's reign. Rather, he was seeking to discredit the Jacobean system of government, in which Court factions were prominently involved, that had led to his own downfall [68]. He therefore cast around for a period in English history which could provide an alternative model, and he believed he had found it in the reign of the first Tudor. Yet although many of the key documents which would shed light on the politics of this period have been lost, there is considerable evidence of the existence of factional intrigue at the Court of Henry VII. Episodes such as the arrest and fine of the Archbishop of York in 1495; the disgrace of Sir Richard Guildford, Councillor and Comptroller of the household, in 1505; and the sudden resignation of the Attorney-General, Sir James Hobart, in 1507, suggest that there was such a phenomenon as 'Court politics' under Henry VII, and that it produced a number of significant casualties.

Gunn's findings have now been reinforced by Professor Davies, in a study of the Croft family of Herefordshire [80]. Under Henry VII, the head of the family, Sir Richard Croft, was Treasurer of the household until 1494 and steward to Prince Arthur until the latter's death in 1502. His greatest enemy was another leading member of the royal household, the Lord Chamberlain, Sir William Stanley, whose lands bordered his. The supporters of both men were engaged in some sort of violent confrontation in Herefordshire in 1487, and this, suggests Davies, may be the background to the passing of an Act [*Doc.* 9] establishing procedures for investigating and trying household officers who conspired to murder either the King, his Councillors, or their fellow officers. This shows that the Court was far from being a place where there was no politics. On the contrary, it was an arena in which personal and factional struggles were bitterly fought out.

Clear evidence of this came in 1495–96 with the downfall of the Lord Chamberlain, Sir William Stanley, who was in treasonable communication with the pretender Perkin Warbeck (see below, p. 82). So also was John Radcliffe, Lord FitzWalter, a former Lord Steward. Dr Starkey has suggested that the discovery of treason at the heart of the royal household may have prompted a significant change in the organisation of the Chamber. This involved separating off the Privy Chamber, which now became distinct from both the Presence Chamber – where the throne was located and where the King met his Council and received important visitors – and the Guard Chamber, where his bodyguard was stationed [69]. The Privy Chamber staff was tiny, consisting merely of the Groom of the Stool and six other grooms, but they were the only persons who had a right of entry. Not even the principal household officers could claim admission to what was now truly Henry's inner sanctum.

Starkey's suggestion that Stanley's fall from office in early 1495 and the separation of the Privy Chamber were cause and effect has been challenged by Dr Gunn, on the grounds that a household ordinance of 1493 provides evidence that the Privy Chamber already had an autonomous existence [68]. But it may well be that Henry's doubts about his Lord Chamberlain's loyalty predated his actual fall, for Stanley's conduct over many years had demonstrated both his ambition and his capacity for causing trouble (see below, p. 39). Henry's distrust of Stanley could well have caused him to take steps to improve his security in the early 1490s. In other words, Starkey's suggestion of a link between Stanley's conduct and the separating-out of the Privy Chamber may be correct, even if the date has to be advanced by several years.

THE COMMON LAW AND CHANCERY

The two principal courts of common law were the King's Bench and Common Pleas. Each of these was presided over by a Chief Justice, assisted by a number of lesser or 'puisne' judges, and they held their sessions in the great hall of the palace of Westminster. They sat during the four legal terms only, and since a term lasted no more than three weeks it meant that justice could be done for a mere three months a year. This limited provision was further restricted by the fact that the judges sat for only three hours a day and that the lawyers made extensive use in their pleadings of Norman French – a bastard language which by Henry VII's time was incomprehensible to anyone outside the legal profession. However, twice a year the judges of the central courts set out on the assizes which took them to the principal county towns, where they dealt with cases remitted to them by the local Justices of the Peace.

The law was a profession which was highly regarded and could bring rich rewards to its practitioners. Not all lawyers practised in London. Many found employment in manorial or Church courts or as clerks to JPs. And of those who were based in London a significant number went into the King's service. This was particularly the case during the reign of Edward IV, who created the new office of Solicitor-General to supplement that of Attorney-General which had been instituted under Henry VI. About one-third of all the non-noble members of Edward's Council were lawyers, and the proportion was even greater under Henry VII [75].

When a plaintiff decided to initiate an action in King's Bench or Common Pleas he had to purchase a writ. In theory, the forms of writ were limited to those which had obtained in Edward I's day, but in practice, and largely through the use of legal fictions, there was considerable flexibility [70]. However, a minor inaccuracy in a writ could invalidate the whole case, and defence lawyers were skilled in the use of technicalities to delay proceedings. Even a straightforward case might take as long as eighteen months, and more complicated ones could drag on for several years. In assize courts and Quarter Sessions (see below, pp. 46–7) persons accused of committing an offence were usually presented for trial by a grand jury, consisting of the more substantial inhabitants of the locality. The assumption behind this procedure was that such men would be likely to have personal knowledge of the accused and to know whether the charges against him were well founded. Only if they approved of the bill of indictment would the case go ahead.

However, the indictment of an offender was merely the first stage in bringing him to trial. He had first to be apprehended, and this was not always easy. There was no police force in Tudor England, and parish constables varied in ability and were lacking in resources. Even when offenders were pursued by the sheriff and his officers, they could claim sanctuary in parish churches, churchyards, and a large number of other places. In the unlikely event of their actually being arrested they still had a good chance of escaping justice. Those who had even a minimum degree of literacy could claim benefit of clergy (see below, p. 63). Others might have to be released because the indictment against them contained a technical inaccuracy such as the mis-spelling of a name. Even if they were brought to trial, there was no certainty that justice would be done. Twelve men would be chosen by the sheriff to form the trial jury, but they were drawn from a lower social level than grand jurymen and were therefore more susceptible to bribery, intimidation and blackmail from interested parties. Assuming that they found the accused guilty, there was only a small chance that he would undergo the prescribed punishment. All too frequently he would simply disappear, and although the courts could resort to an ascending hierarchy of fulminations, culminating in a declaration of outlawry, these were rarely effective. Indeed, one of the reasons why Henry VII created the office of Surveyor of the King's Prerogative (see above, p. 18) was to improve the procedures for rounding-up outlaws and thereby restore confidence in the functioning of the common-law system.

Henry also tried to check the abuse of juries, through two statutes passed by the 1495 Parliament. The first of these required Justices of the Peace to watch over the sheriff when he empanelled juries, while the second authorised them to dispense with juries of presentment in certain cases. It may be doubted whether either of these statutes achieved its purpose, for the facts of life in early Tudor England were such that local magnates were far better placed to get their way – even if this involved perverting the course of justice – than the agents of the distant King. Magnate power derived in large part from the practice of retaining, for a lord with liveried retainers in his service had, in the words of one of Henry VII's judges, 'a great company at his command. And for this [reason] men do not dare to execute the law on any of them' [73 *p. 92*]. There was already in existence a statute of 1468 forbidding the retaining of anyone except menial servants, but since it excluded retaining for 'lawful purposes' it did not, in practice, apply to peers, who were likely to be the worst offenders [*Doc. 12*]. In November 1485 the members of Henry VII's first Parliament, Commons as well as Lords, swore the oath prescribed under the 1468 statute by which they bound themselves not to 'retain any man by indenture or oath, or give livery, sign or token contrary to the law'. The value of such a promise, however solemnly affirmed, was limited, as Sir William Hussey, Chief Justice of the King's Bench, made plain. He recalled how a similar ceremony had taken place in Edward IV's reign, yet 'he saw, within an hour, while they were in the Star Chamber, divers of the lords make retainments by oath and surety and other things which were directly contrary to their said ... oaths' [73 *p. 91*].

Henry VII never attempted to ban retaining altogether. Even if such a step had been practicable, it would have been unwise, for in the absence of any police force or standing army the King depended upon his greater subjects for the maintenance of public order and the government of their localities, and they could only act effectively because they had private armies of retainers at their disposal. Henry positively encouraged retaining when it was to his advantage to do so. This was the case with his trusted servant Sir Thomas Lovell, whom he appointed Keeper of Sherwood Forest and Constable of Nottingham Castle, thereby enabling him to retain some 1,400 men for his own (and the crown's) service. Although Henry secured legislation against illegal retaining as early as 1487, it was not until 1504, when his fears for the succession were growing, that he took firm action to curb the worst excesses of the practice. By a statute of that year, all those who had retainers were required to submit a list of their names to the King and obtain a licence from him [*Doc. 13*]. No exceptions were permitted, and among those indicted for illegal retaining in 1504 were Henry's mother, the Countess of Richmond, and his close confidant and friend, the Earl of Oxford.

Only one peer was brought before a common-law court on a charge of retaining in Henry VII's reign. This was Lord Bergavenny (Abergavenny), who in 1507 was accused in King's Bench of having retained 471 men for 30 months and binding them 'to do both on foot and on horse, lawfully and unlawfully' whatever he commanded [73]. The court found Bergavenny guilty and imposed the penalty prescribed in the 1468 statute – namely, 100 shillings (£5) for each month for which each man was unlawfully retained. This amounted to a fine of £70,650, a sum far greater than the entire capital value of Bergavenny's English estates, yet which was increased to around £100,000 after Henry made the unfortunate peer give recognisances for good behaviour [*Doc. 14*]. Happily for Bergavenny, Henry condescended to accept a mere £5,000, to be paid in ten annual instalments, but the King retained the right to demand full payment if and when he saw fit. At first sight the treatment meted out to Bergavenny seems extremely harsh, for others were no less guilty of illegal retaining than he, but did not suffer in similar manner. Henry, however, had reason to believe that Bergavenny had wavered in his loyalty during the Western Rebellion of 1497 (see below, p. 43), and it could have been for this reason that he determined to make him an example by prosecuting him to the full extent of the law [93].

Despite the legislation of 1504, there was no sudden transformation in the practice of retaining, and disorder, for which retaining was in large part responsible, continued to be a problem for Henry's successors. Yet his efforts to set bounds on retaining had a measure of success even in his own lifetime, and he established the principle which later Tudors put into effect.

Although the common law was designed to protect property, more and more property cases were going to the court of Chancery in the late fifteenth century. This was because Chancery, unlike Common

Pleas, took cognisance of trusts or 'uses' and also of commercial contracts. In the closing years of Henry VI's reign, Chancery had handled some 140 cases a year, compared with just under 80 for the Exchequer, 1,600 for King's Bench, and 13,500 for Common Pleas. Under Edward IV this figure rose to 550, and by the time Henry VII died Chancery was dealing with some 600 cases a year and was clearly established as one of the four central courts of the kingdom [76].

As Chancery was increasingly called upon to deal with complex disputes, it needed to expand its range of expertise. Down to the mid-fifteenth century it had been staffed principally by clerics with a theological qualification. Morton's appointment as Master of the Rolls in 1473 marked a watershed, for he was a Doctor of Civil Law, and from then onwards the personnel of Chancery was drawn mainly from graduates in civil (Roman) law, many of them straight down from university. Their professionalism increased the effectiveness and therefore the popularity of the court. Its growing prestige also reflected the changing position of the Lord Chancellor, who was now emerging as the King's chief minister. As such, he commanded an authority which could not be matched by the Chief Justices of King's Bench and Common Pleas, despite the fact that their long-established courts dealt with many more cases than the upstart Chancery [76].

6 REGIONAL GOVERNMENT

The restoration of the royal finances under Henry VII depended heavily upon the exploitation of land revenues. It is therefore understandable that the first Tudor was reluctant to part with any of his estates in order to endow new nobles. Apart from his uncle, Jasper Tudor, whom he made Duke of Bedford, and his sons Arthur and Henry, who became Dukes of Cornwall and York respectively, Henry created no new dukes and only three earls (of Bath, Derby, and Devon). The most that members of his affinity could reasonably hope for was appointment to the Order of the Garter – a great honour, of course, but not hereditary – and of nearly 40 new Knights of the Garter appointed in Henry's reign, more than half were men who had served him in government.

However, there may be another reason why Henry was reluctant to confer hereditary titles on his followers. Many of the problems that the monarchy had faced over the previous century had stemmed from the fact that the nobility was too powerful, and Edward IV had exacerbated this problem by substantially increasing the peerage. Henry seems deliberately to have adopted the opposite policy – namely, a drastic reduction in the number of lords temporal, with a consequent diminution of their military power and territorial influence. Whereas at Henry's accession there were twenty dukes, marquesses and earls, there were only one duke and nine earls at the time of his death. One reason for this shrinkage is that a number of aristocratic families died out in the male line during the course of the reign, leading to the disappearance of one duke (Bedford) and three earls (Huntingdon, Rivers and Wiltshire). But Henry made no attempt to fill the gaps created by natural causes. On the contrary, he aided the decline. For instance, in 1489 he agreed to advance the Earl of Nottingham to the rank of marquess (of Berkeley), but only on condition that he disinherited his brother.

At Nottingham's death, therefore, the earldom became extinct, as did the marquessate [93]. The ranks of the higher nobility were further thinned by the execution of the Earl of Warwick in 1499 and the death in battle of the Earl of Lincoln in 1487.

Henry's reluctance to create new peerages, in order to limit the power of the aristocracy, caused resentment. Nobody had played a more important part in winning the crown for Henry than his step-uncle, Sir William Stanley, but although he was appointed Lord Chamberlain of the royal household and Chief Justice of North Wales he was not given a peerage – whereas his brother, Lord Stanley, was made Earl of Derby. During the late 1480s Sir William gave notice of his ambitions and expectations by briefly incorporating into his heraldic device the wolf's-head badge of the Earldom of Chester. However, this particular title was traditionally reserved for the eldest son of the sovereign, and was duly conferred on Prince Arthur in 1489. Stanley's anger at being denied a peerage may have been fuelled by Henry's failure to grant him any royal lands with which to augment his estates in Lancashire and North Wales [90]. In 1487 he attempted to extend his influence into Shropshire and Herefordshire, but was apparently thwarted by the region's leading magnate, Sir Richard Croft, who was Treasurer of Henry's household [80]. Frustrated in his territorial and social ambitions, and worried about the security of his existing estates, it was doubtless a bitter and resentful Stanley who was later indicted of having entered into a treasonable correspondence with the pretender Perkin Warbeck, for which he was executed in 1495.

Henry's long-term objective of reducing the numbers and role of the greater nobility raised important questions about how the country was to be ruled. Given the lack of resources at the crown's disposal, it is hardly surprising that successive monarchs had become dependent upon the magnates for the maintenance of order in the localities. However, the disadvantages inherent in this system of devolved government had been exposed only too clearly during the civil wars that dominated the period 1455–85, for it was frequently the very men in whom the King had placed his trust who were themselves the instigators of disorder and rebellion. During his years of exile in France, Henry had been able to study at first hand the working of a more autocratic method of government, and the Spanish ambassador, writing home in 1498, declared that Henry 'would like to govern England in the French fashion' [6 *p. 178*]. The ambassador added his opinion, however, that 'he cannot', thereby acknowledging what most historians now accept, that Henry was subject to the same limitations as his predecessors. He simply did not have the means to set up and maintain a system of tight royal control over the localities, nor could he afford a standing army to impose his will on recalcitrant magnates. The only military forces permanently at Henry's disposal were 200 or so Yeomen of the Guard and a handful of mercenaries. He also had, at Calais, a garrison of some 800 men, which was considered very large and cost £10,000 a year to maintain – though this charge, fortunately for Henry, was borne directly by the Company of the Staple, who used Calais as their entrepôt. Whenever troops were needed on a large scale, Henry had to issue commissions of array to the principal figures in every county, ordering them to levy men for his service.

Henry, then, had to rely for the governance of the localities on a handful of magnates. In Essex and East Anglia he depended upon his Lord Great Chamberlain, the thirteenth Earl of Oxford, who had shared his exile. Oxford carried out his functions efficiently, and although in 1504 he was heavily fined for illegal retaining, he never betrayed the King's trust. In the south-west Henry looked to another companion of his exile, Sir Giles Daubeney, a native of Somerset, whom he made a baron in 1486 and a Knight of the Garter in 1487. Eight years later, following the execution of Sir William Stanley, Daubeney took his place as Lord Chamberlain of the royal household. Like Oxford, Daubeney served the King faithfully, though in 1497 his close links with a number of local families apparently caused him to hesitate before carrying out Henry's orders to crush the Western Rebellion [92].

While Oxford and Daubeney had demonstrated their loyalty to Henry even before he seized the throne, there were other nobles who served the King as *de facto* regional governors who had earlier been prominent Yorkists. One member of this group was Henry Percy, fourth Earl of Northumberland; another was Thomas Howard, Earl of Surrey. At the beginning of Henry's reign the principal magnate in the north-east was Northumberland [89]. He possessed what was 'probably the largest private army in England' [93 *p. 74*] and had fielded some 3,000 troops under Richard III's banner at Bosworth. Although he took no part in the battle, and it was widely believed that if he had done so it would have been against rather than for Richard, he was briefly imprisoned by the new King. However, the outbreak of disturbances in the north prompted Henry to order the Earl's release in December 1485 and his restoration as Warden of both the East and Middle Marches – offices of great military significance. Henry took the precaution of making Northumberland swear a special oath of allegiance, give surety for his good behaviour, and hold his wardenships only for a year at a time, but it turned out that his trust in the Earl was justified. While the King was on progress in the north in the spring of 1486, Northumberland apparently foiled a plot masterminded by Francis, Lord Lovell, to seize Henry at York. Furthermore, in June 1487 he held aloof from the supporters of the pretender, Lambert Simnel, who had crossed the Irish Sea and landed in Lancashire. Northumberland's unexpected death in April 1489, at the hands of a mob protesting against the collection of a parliamentary subsidy, seems to have shocked Henry – not least because it implied that his hold on power was still fragile [86].

Northumberland was replaced as the King's man in the north by the Earl of Surrey. This was partly dictated by the fact that Northumberland's heir, the fifth Earl, was a minor. But Henry did not lose interest in him. On the contrary, he had the boy brought up at Court and made him a Knight of the Bath in 1481 – at the same time as Henry's son, Arthur, was created Prince of Wales – and Knight of the Garter in 1495. The fifth Earl showed his gratitude by serving in the royal army which put an end to the Western Rebellion by crushing the insurgents at Blackheath. In 1503 he was appointed Warden of the East March and, as such, escorted Henry's daughter, Margaret, on her way to Scotland to be married to James IV. Northumberland, as befitted the head of a great noble house, lived in magnificent style, and it was perhaps the fear of Percy influence reasserting itself at a time when a succession crisis might be approaching that prompted Henry, at the very end of his reign, to fine the Earl the massive sum of £10,000, nominally for wrongful disposal of a ward in marriage. It appears that Northumberland had actually paid half this sum before the death of Henry VII freed him from the remaining obligation.

Henry's choice of Surrey to take the fourth Earl of Northumberland's place in the north is at first sight surprising. The Earl had fought against Henry at Bosworth, alongside his father, the Duke of Norfolk, who had been killed in the battle. He was subsequently imprisoned in the Tower and his valuable East Anglian estates were confiscated by Act of attainder. Moreover, he was denied the right to succeed to his father's title. Surrey, then, had good grounds for resentment, but Henry calculated that he might seize the opportunity, if it was offered, to restore his fortunes by serving the new King [94]. The fact that the Howards held little or no property in northern England meant that Surrey would be less of a potential threat to royal authority than was the case with the Percies; and his lack of local connections was a positive advantage, since this would enable him to administer justice impartially, instead of, as hitherto, in the Percies' favour. Henry therefore released Surrey from imprisonment in 1489 and gave him a senior command in the large army assembled to put down the Yorkshire rebellion. Subsequently, Surrey took Northumberland's place as governor of the border regions with Scotland.

Henry's decision to entrust men like Northumberland and Surrey with key roles in regional government came from the recognition that he needed to form a broad basis of support among the peerage if his regime was to survive and the localities were to be well governed. Nevertheless, he was quite prepared to clip the wings of individual noblemen if he did not trust them. Among those peers who found their local influence sharply diminished after the accession of the first Tudor was Ralph Neville, third Earl of Westmorland. Westmorland had been closely associated with Richard III, and was briefly imprisoned when Henry VII seized the crown. Although he was soon released, in order that he could continue governing County Durham, Henry seems not to have trusted him. Westmorland was deprived of valuable lands and annuities which he had received during Richard's reign, and was ordered to place his eldest son under the King's guardianship. It was perhaps as a consequence of Henry's suspicious attitude that Westmorland sometimes appeared to be lukewarm in his support for the Tudor monarchy – he was, for instance, conspicuously absent from the force which Henry assembled in 1489 to restore order in Yorkshire. On the other hand, he resisted any temptation to throw in his lot with Lambert Simnel in 1487, and he was given a command in the army which Henry raised to invade Scotland ten years later. Although Westmorland, perforce, remained the principal lay peer in County Durham, it was doubtless with an eye to reducing – or at least limiting – his influence there that in 1494 Henry appointed his trusted adviser and Lord Privy Seal, Richard Fox, as Bishop of Durham.

In a number of areas, where there was no major nobleman in place at the beginning of his reign, Henry selected members of the gentry to exercise regional power. As already mentioned, Shropshire and Herefordshire were dominated by the Treasurer of Henry's household, Sir Richard Croft, while in Oxfordshire – which witnessed a small-scale rebellion in 1486 led by the followers of Viscount Lovell – Henry conferred authority on a Buckinghamshire gentleman, Edmund Hampden. Though Hampden's presence initially proved unpopular with the local gentry, provoking an outbreak of disorder in 1494, the county was pacified by the mid-1490s and does not seem to have suffered from the lack of a nobleman as administrator [82; 91].

Henry, then, was not wedded exclusively to one model of regional government but was willing to give key roles to members of the gentry as well as the peerage. However, despite this flexible approach, Henry committed some serious errors of judgement in the way he distributed power at the local level, and, as a result, his competence as a ruler has recently been called into question. Perhaps the most striking of his policy failures occurred in the south and west of England, comprising the six counties of Cornwall, Devonshire, Somerset, Wiltshire, Dorset and Hampshire. Apart from Hampshire, this region was dominated by three peers – namely, the Earl of Devon; Giles, Lord Daubeney; and Robert, Lord Willoughby de Broke – even though many of its leading gentry, such as Nicholas Latimer of Duntish in Dorset and Hugh Luttrell of Dunster in Somerset, had provided the core of Henry's support in England at his accession. The exclusion from office of the region's gentry, who had expected to be rewarded for their loyalty, drove many of them to rebellion in 1497, and those who did not themselves take up arms did little or nothing to impede the rebel advance towards London [82; 92]. The rebel gentry were joined by James, Lord Audley, who until 1486 had been the only peer resident in Somerset. He too had been excluded by Henry from the government of his locality, perhaps because his father had been Richard III's Lord Treasurer. Led by Audley, the rebel army came perilously close to achieving its objective, for it reached Blackheath, on the outskirts of London, before it was encountered and defeated by Henry's forces.

Henry's decision to concentrate power in too few hands in the south and west helped precipitate perhaps the most serious crisis of his reign. By taking the loyalty of the region's gentry for granted, instead of rewarding them for their devotion, Henry provoked opposition from a quarter where he least expected it. Yet if the lesson of the Western Rebellion was that power and authority in the localities needed to be more widely diffused, evidence from Warwickshire and the North Midlands shows that the process of diffusion could not be allowed to go too far. This region lacked a dominant figure, because one of its two leading nobles, the Duke of Buckingham, was still a minor, while the other, the Earl of Warwick, remained a prisoner in the Tower until his execution in

1499. The crown, which already possessed substantial Duchy of Lancaster estates in the area, took control of Warwick's property and thereby established itself as the greatest regional landowner. Henry might well have chosen to rule through a newly created Tudor peer, but instead he allowed his authority to be distributed among the lesser nobles and greater gentry.

Henry's failure to install a powerful figure in the North Midlands proved disastrous, for it meant there was no one powerful enough to impose a peaceful settlement when Sir Henry Willoughby launched an attack on the Derbyshire and Nottinghamshire lands of his neighbour, Lord Grey of Codnor, in January 1488. The King was so alarmed at the breakdown of law and order in the region that he even considered freeing Warwick and restoring him to his estates. This would have been too risky, however, and Henry therefore took the simpler course of forcing Willoughby and Grey to enter mutual recognisances for keeping the peace. But this did not prevent a recrudescence of violence the following year, when Willoughby's retainers were involved in a large-scale affray at Lichfield [79].

Henry's subsequent attempts to impose order on the North Midlands were ill-judged and counter-productive. In 1492–93 he increased the influence of the Stanley family in the area by appointing Humphrey Stanley as steward of Tutbury and sheriff of Staffordshire. But Stanley behaved even more outrageously than Willoughby had done, for in 1494, while still sheriff, he was involved in the murder of a local landowner. This incident tarnished royal authority, particularly since Stanley went unpunished. It was not until 1502–4 that Henry appointed a new steward of Tutbury, overhauled the membership of the Commission of the Peace to include a greater number of local gentry, and elevated the Vernon family to help fill the power vacuum which had existed since the beginning of his reign. He appears to have been aided by his mother, Lady Margaret Beaufort, who held the manor of Collyweston in Northamptonshire. There she established an unofficial council which, from 1499 to 1505, helped restore and maintain order in the Midlands [26].

If the Western Rebellion demonstrated the folly of allowing power to be monopolised by a handful of peers, the disorders in Warwickshire and adjoining areas served to underscore the importance of magnates in regional government. A dominant figure, drawn either from the nobility or greater gentry, was clearly an essential ingredient in achieving stable and firm rule in the localities, as was the involvement of the lesser gentry. Other factors, including luck, also had a part to play. In the north, for example, Henry's appointment of the Earl of Surrey as his lieutenant was only one element in the process of pacification. Perkin Warbeck, oddly enough, was another, for in return for Scottish military assistance in 1497 he promised to cede Berwick to James IV [83]. Local inhabitants were appalled at this threat to their security, and therefore rallied behind Henry. This made Surrey's task much easier, and by 1501 – when he returned to London to take up office as Lord Treasurer – the north was relatively quiet [83].

Henry was aided by the fact that he was, in his own right, Earl of Richmond in Yorkshire, and one of the banners under which he fought at Bosworth sported the image of a pied bull, the 'Dun Cow', which was the badge of his earldom [83]. The new King also won support by his lenient treatment of those northerners who joined the pretender, Lambert Simnel, in 1487. These included Lord Scrope of Masham and Lord Scrope of Bolton, both of whom were pardoned after compounding with Henry. Another of Simnel's adherents, Sir Edmund Hastings of Roxby, escaped with a warning and was not only allowed to retain the stewardship of Pickering but was appointed as the King's financial agent in the Yorkshire district of Richmondshire, which was the opening to great wealth. In the words of Dr Pollard, 'the King's clemency proved effective policy' [83 *p. 383*].

As well as the 'Dun Cow', Henry's banners at Bosworth carried the image of the red dragon, to emphasise his descent from the ancient Kings of Wales and Britain [85]. He later chose this symbol as one of the supporters of the royal arms, and also gave it a prominent place on his coinage. Henry was proud of his Welsh ancestry, yet in fact he was only a quarter Welsh [40] and in practice he was preoccupied, as King, with English affairs. After the creation of his eldest son, Arthur, as Prince of Wales in 1489, he followed Edward IV's example by appointing a council to rule the principality in the boy's name, under the direction of Henry's uncle, Jasper Tudor, Duke of Bedford. It was charged with overseeing the administration of justice and ensuring that the law was enforced. As far as the marcher lordships were concerned, the majority of these had passed into royal hands, but whether or not the marcher lords were his deputies, Henry used recognisances to bind them and their stewards, under the threat of financial penalties, to keep the peace and maintain order. Wales was different from most of the English counties in that there was no major peer whom Henry could use as his agent in government, particularly after Bedford's death in 1495. The Herberts were great landowners in Wales, but their property had passed into the hands of a female heir, Elizabeth Herbert. However, in 1491 Henry facilitated a marriage between Elizabeth and one of his close associates, Sir Charles Somerset (see above, p. 25). He then created Somerset Lord Herbert and built up his influence in the region by granting him leases of crown lands as well as local offices.

Generally speaking, it seems that while Henry did have an overall strategy designed to restrict the numbers and influence of the greater nobility in his kingdom, and was prepared to employ members of the gentry to govern in their place in certain areas, he nevertheless accepted the need to preserve aristocratic power in most localities. There is nothing surprising about Henry's use of traditional methods to maintain order. Given his limited resources and the need to win support among the political nation for the newly established Tudor dynasty, he had little scope for radical innovation.

JUSTICES OF THE PEACE

Sir William Hussey, speaking to his fellow judges in the first year of Henry VII's reign, declared that 'the laws will never be well executed until all the lords spiritual and temporal are of one accord to execute them effectually, and when the King on his part and the lords on their part both want to do this and do it' [22 *p*. 77]. There could be no doubting the King's desire to see the laws put into execution, but he depended for this on the Justices of the Peace, appointed annually from among the leading gentry of every shire, and charged by the Commission of the Peace with the responsibility for maintaining order in their localities. Their duties were substantially increased by statute during the Tudor period, and Henry VII's reign saw an Act of 1487 giving them authority to take bail, and the one of 1495, already mentioned, making it lawful for them to act upon information received without waiting for formal indictment by a grand jury.

Much of the Justices' work was done by a handful of them coming together as the needs of their situation and their own convenience dictated. But four times a year formal Quarter Sessions were held, at which all the Justices were supposed to be present and which were also attended by most persons of consequence in the shire. At these Sessions the JPs tried all those indicted of any crime except treason – which was always investigated by the Council –

and either passed sentence themselves or, in difficult cases, remitted the case for consideration by the assize judges (see above, p. 33).

The Justices of the Peace were not simply judicial officers. They were also responsible for supervising the administration of their shires, and at Quarter Sessions they enquired into the conduct of all local officials, including mayors and sheriffs. Parliament added to their duties in this respect, as by an Act of 1495 which required them to suppress unlawful games and to control alehouses. The regulation of economic activity, which had previously been the concern of the manorial courts or of the old popular courts of the shire and hundred, was also being taken over by the JPs, and here again Parliament added to their burden. In 1504, to give merely one example, they were charged with seeing that pewter and brass were of the specified degree of fineness.

Not all JPs were impartial servants of the crown. Many used their offices to pursue private vendettas, thereby adding to lawlessness rather than curbing it. Henry could always remove unsatisfactory Justices from the Commission of the Peace, but he might well have problems in replacing them, for the number of men of substance in any shire was quite small. Delinquent JPs could be summoned before Chancery or the common-law courts, and King's Bench could annul decisions taken at Quarter Sessions if it thought the Justices had failed to carry out their duties. A statute of 1489 required JPs to read out a proclamation at Quarter Sessions clearly defining their powers. It also made provision for anyone with a grievance to take his complaint either to the assize judges or direct to the King. Such primitive and clumsy machinery was not, however, very effective, and the Act should be regarded more as an expression of intent than an actual remedy.

While the King needed the co-operation of the JPs to maintain order in the countryside, the Justices themselves were dependent upon lesser officials to bring offenders to book. Every hundred was obliged to provide itself with a high constable, and every parish with a petty constable, and these appointments were usually made by the JPs. Constables had no police force to back them up and ran considerable risks. Not surprisingly, there were few volunteers for such posts, and JPs frequently had to use their powers of compulsion in order to fill them. The consequence was that at the lowest levels of society, where the agents of law and order came into direct contact with lawlessness and disorder, there was a lack of will and means, and a great deal of crime went unpunished.

IRELAND

If the involvement of members of the nobility in the governance of the localities was highly desirable for the maintenance of order and royal authority in England, it was essential in Ireland. Though Henry VII was nominally Lord of Ireland, in practice English rule was confined to the 'Pale' – a strip of coast some twenty miles wide and fifty miles long, stretching from just south of Dublin northwards to Dundalk. Beyond the Pale, the real rulers of Ireland were the descendants of the Anglo-Norman invaders of the twelfth century. Only three of these – Desmond, Kildare and Ormond – owned sufficient territory to have acquired the rank of earl. Unless Henry was prepared to rule Ireland directly, which would mean maintaining an expensive bureaucracy and army, he would have to rely on one of these magnates to act as his Lord Deputy. His choice was limited by the fact that successive Earls of Desmond had sworn never again to enter a walled city, following the execution of the seventh Earl in 1468. Henry might have preferred the Butlers, Earls of Ormond, who had been loyal Lancastrians, but they had been enforced absentees from Ireland ever since the execution of the fifth Earl in 1461. Even after Henry's accession the seventh Earl of Ormond preferred to continue living in England, where he was appointed Chamberlain to the Queen and given an English peerage, rather than return to Ireland. This left Henry dependent on Gerald FitzGerald, eighth Earl of Kildare, who had held office as Lord Deputy under the Yorkists. As head of the influential Geraldine family and lord of more than half the Pale, Kildare was a power to be reckoned with.

It was of vital importance to English security and the continuation of the Tudor dynasty that Ireland should not be used as a springboard for the invasion of England by Yorkist pretenders. The best way to do this was by reaching an accommodation with Kildare as quickly as possible, but it was only in March 1486 that Henry appointed his uncle, Jasper Tudor, Duke of Bedford, as Lord Lieutenant of Ireland, at the same time confirming Kildare in his post as Lord Deputy. Henry also summoned Kildare to England, ostensibly to advise him on Irish affairs, but Kildare, scenting a trap, demanded letters of safe conduct signed by members of the English nobility as well as the King. Henry rejected this implied claim that he could not be trusted, so Kildare ignored the royal summons and remained in Ireland.

If Henry was indeed contemplating Kildare's removal, possibly in favour of Ormond, he had committed a serious tactical blunder, for later in 1486 the pretender, Lambert Simnel, arrived in Ireland (see below, p. 75), and Kildare, feeling his position threatened, let his brother, the Irish Chancellor, Sir Thomas FitzGerald, take Simnel under his wing. In 1487 Kildare came out openly in favour of the pretender by allowing him to be crowned as 'Edward VI' in Dublin Cathedral and accepting a commission from him as Lord Lieutenant. Simnel's subsequent defeat and capture at Stoke put an end to whatever hopes Kildare may have had, but Henry was left with the problem of how to deal with him at a time when the deepening crisis in Brittany (see below, pp. 76–7) demanded his urgent attention. He could not risk removing Kildare from office for fear that Ireland might become ungovernable. He therefore sent Sir Richard Edgecumbe to Dublin in July 1488, with several hundred troops and instructions to secure new oaths of loyalty from the Irish nobles and gentry [97].

In the short run, Henry's lenient treatment of Kildare seemed to have paid dividends. Early in 1489 the Lord Deputy and a number of other Anglo-Irish peers were invited to Greenwich, where Henry laid on a magnificent feast in their honour, but provided a piquant reminder of their lack of judgement by having Lambert Simnel wait on them at table. However, Kildare was far from reconciled to Tudor rule, and when the Yorkist pretender, Perkin Warbeck, landed in Ireland in October 1491 (see below, p. 80), the Deputy took no action against him. Henry now despatched a small force to Ireland, which co-operated with the Butlers, sworn enemies of the Geraldines, to remove Kildare from office. This did not solve Henry's problems, however. Rather, it added to them, for the removal of Kildare was followed by a period of acute disorder, as the Butlers and Geraldines fought each other [97]. Warbeck was now in Burgundy, but there was always the danger that he would reappear in Ireland with Burgundian or French help to challenge Henry's hold on the English throne. Although Henry, in November 1492, had apparently restored good relations with France by the Treaty of Etaples, he may have remained suspicious of the French king's intentions. After all, it was from Charles VIII that Warbeck had first obtained assistance, and although Charles was now planning to invade Italy it was by no means certain that this would absorb all his energies [101].

Henry wrote to Charles, announcing that he intended to conquer Ireland – an implied warning to France not to intervene. He was as good as his word, for although he appointed his young son, Prince

Henry, as Lord Lieutenant of Ireland, he chose an experienced soldier, Sir Edward Poynings, as his Deputy. Poynings arrived in Ireland in September 1494 with a force of 1,000 men, and immediately set off to suppress a revolt by the Gaelic Irish which had broken out in Ulster. He was accompanied by Kildare, but soon became convinced that the Earl was in touch with the rebels and encouraging their resistance. He therefore arrested Kildare and took him to Drogheda, where he was attainted by the Irish Parliament and sent prisoner to England. In taking such drastic action against Kildare, Poynings had to abandon his aim of conquering the Gaelic Irish, for he could no longer rely on the Earl's followers to defend the Pale while he was away fighting [100]. Kildare's removal from the scene meant that he could not take advantage of Warbeck's reappearance in Ireland in July 1495 (see below, p. 82). But the pretender won the support of the Earl of Desmond, and together they laid siege to Waterford, the second most important town in the country. Unfortunately for Warbeck, it held out long enough for Poynings to march to its relief, and the pretender had to cut his losses and flee to Scotland.

The attainder of Kildare was one of a number of significant measures enacted by the Drogheda Parliament. Its activities culminated in the passing of the statute known as 'Poynings' Law' which laid down that in future no Irish Parliament should meet or pass legislation without the prior approval of the English government. It has recently been suggested that one of the main purposes of this Act was to make it 'difficult for Warbeck to obtain, as Simnel had, parliamentary approval for his rebellion' [101 *p. 21*]. Members of the Drogheda Parliament were also called upon to help meet the costs of Poynings' expedition, for these were substantial. Between August 1494 and December 1495 the Chamber had disbursed more than £11,700 for this purpose – a sum which represented at least 10 per cent of the King's entire annual income [99]. However, although Poynings succeeded in obtaining from the Drogheda Parliament a vote of five annual subsidies at double the usual rate, and also in reforming the administration of the Irish Customs and thereby increasing their yield, Ireland was still costing Henry some £7,000 a year. Such a burden was not tolerable except in the short term, and Henry therefore recalled Poynings to England in January 1496.

The King had come to realise that in Ireland, if not always in England, local government by a loyal magnate was the cheapest and most efficient solution. Kildare was hardly a model of loyalty, but as an attainted person his lands were now at the King's mercy, and the need for self-preservation predisposed him towards a deal. This was made easier by the fact that during Kildare's enforced stay in England he and the King had learned to like and respect each other. Henry had the Earl's attainder reversed by the English Parliament, and in March 1496 he promoted a marriage between Kildare and Elizabeth St John, the King's second cousin. Henry was now so impressed with Kildare that when it was pointed out to him that 'All England cannot rule yonder gentleman' he replied, 'No? Then he is mete to rule all Ireland' [97 *p. 645*]. Kildare was now reinstated as Lord Deputy, though the King kept possession of his eldest son as surety for his good behaviour. The effects of this change of course were dramatic. The rebel Gaelic chieftains quickly made peace and swore fealty to Henry, and when Warbeck put in yet another appearance – this time at Cork, in July 1497 (see below, p. 88) – Kildare kept his distance. Warbeck sailed off to Cornwall, and for the rest of Henry's reign Ireland, under Kildare, caused the King little trouble. In the words of Steven Ellis, 'in so far as the problem of governing a distant border province a fortnight's journey away from the centre of power was soluble in this age of personal monarchy, Henry VII had solved his Irish problem' [100 *p. 86*].

7 GREAT COUNCILS AND PARLIAMENTS

GREAT COUNCILS

The Great Council, or *magnum concilium*, had roots that went back deep into the Middle Ages. It took the form of a meeting between the King and the lords spiritual and temporal who were his 'natural' advisers. Great Councils had been relatively frequent during the fourteenth and fifteenth centuries, and there were at least fourteen during the reign of Edward IV. Under Henry VII there were four or five, of which two included representatives of the urban communities as well as the peers. The King seems to have summoned Great Councils at times when there were particularly difficult questions affecting the security of the state to be considered. In 1487, for example, there was the threat from the pretender Lambert Simnel in Ireland; in 1488 and 1491 the intractable problem of Brittany demanded immediate attention; while in 1496 the Council was called upon to decide how to respond to the challenge from Perkin Warbeck and the Scots [105].

The advantage of a Great Council from Henry's point of view was that it could focus upon political issues without being distracted by legislation. Furthermore, it could anticipate the proceeds of parliamentary taxation by authorising the immediate raising of money. Great Councils were not an alternative to Parliaments. On the contrary, they were nearly always the prelude to a meeting of Parliament, and it seems highly likely that decisions to summon Parliament were actually taken in prior sessions of the Great Council. Since the peers who met together in the Great Council also had seats in the House of Lords, and since the urban representatives usually fulfilled the same function in the House of Commons, there was a considerable overlap between membership of the Great Council and Parliament. This meant that decisions arrived at in the Great Council were assured of confirmation by the subsequent, larger assembly.

When decisions needed taking quickly, a Great Council was a more efficient body than Parliament, particularly since the quality of its membership reinforced the authority of the King. It was the 1491 Great Council which empowered Henry to collect a Benevolence, and although this particular levy was deeply unpopular, the fact that there was no overt protest against it may be due to the element of consent which Henry had taken pains to secure. Great Councils, like Parliaments, were demonstrations of harmony between the monarch and the political nation. They symbolised the fact that the royal will was also, in a sense, the national will, and thereby made it easier for the King to govern, despite the limited means of coercion at his disposal. A similar symbolic function was performed by exceptionally large meetings of the ordinary Council, such as that which took place in 1499, when Henry discussed the linked questions of Warbeck and foreign policy with no less than 65 Councillors. It is perhaps significant that the Great Council met only once, if at all, after 1496, and that there was only one Parliament after 1497. With twelve years on the throne behind him, Henry felt more secure. Or, to put it another way, it was no longer so essential for him to demonstrate the unity of interests between him and his subjects. If Henry did indeed rule more autocratically in the closing decade of his reign, thereby becoming increasingly unpopular, the absence of representative assemblies may be both an indicator and a cause [105].

PARLIAMENT

In early Tudor England Parliament was neither an integral nor a regular part of the machinery of government. Henry VII reigned for 24 years, but during this time he summoned only seven Parliaments, of which five took place in his first ten years as King. All but three of Henry's Parliaments met for one session only, lasting a few weeks at most. Second sessions, when they took place, were equally short. The total time taken up by Parliaments in 1485–1509 was 69 weeks – less than three weeks for each year of Henry's rule. Yet even this figure is misleading, since from 1497 to 1509 there were only two parliaments, which between them lasted for about 120 days. This means that during the second half of Henry's reign parliamentary sessions were equivalent to just over nine days a year.

THE LORDS

The Lords consisted of two estates, the spiritual and the secular. Only thirteen archbishops and bishops and seventeen abbots and priors came to Henry's first Parliament, but in a full house the spiritual peers numbered just under 50. The lay lords were fewer in number, since the heads of many noble families were minors – the result of natural causes, intensified by the Wars of the Roses. As the reign progressed, minors came of age, attainders were reversed, and dormant titles were revived, until there were about 40 lords temporal eligible to sit in the Upper House. But Henry did not summon them all. He was the last English king to exercise the right to exclude those peers of whom he disapproved.

Parliament was still primarily what it had been in the Middle Ages, a meeting of the King and his Councillors with the peers of the realm. The Lords assembled in a room in the royal palace of Westminster, where they were grouped around the throne. The King himself frequently presided, and when he was absent his place was taken by the Lord Chancellor. Near the throne sat the judges and other members of the Council, but they were there as advisers and took no part in debates or voting. It was because non-noble Councillors were unable to play a full part in the Lords' proceedings that many of them preferred to stand for election to the so-called Lower House – a sign that the centre of political power was gradually shifting.

Further evidence of this is provided by the change in the procedure for dealing with bills that took place in Henry VII's reign. At his accession it was still customary for public bills to begin their passage in the Lords. Subsequently, when they were sent down to the Commons, they took precedence over bills that had originated in the Lower House. This practice was still current in 1497 but not in 1504. 'Procedurally speaking', then, as G.R. Elton observed, 'the Parliament of 1497 was the last medieval Parliament' [101, II p. 54]. Elton also points out that although Henry VII continued his predecessors' practice of amending bills after they had completed their passage through both Houses, he was the last English king to do so. One reason for this was the increasing formality of draft parliamentary legislation. From 1504 onwards both Houses worked closely together – often with guidance from royal Councillors – to produce what were, in effect, re-statements of the law. These had to be drawn up and amended with great care, for since Richard III's reign it had become the practice for statutes to be printed. They thereby gained a degree of determinateness and authority which had been lacking in the days of manuscript copies.

THE COMMONS

The Commons were already a House, both in fact and in current phraseology, by the time Henry VII came to the throne, since they had to be called something to distinguish them from the Lords, who in theory *were* Parliament. While the Lords and the King discussed affairs of state in the royal palace, the Commons met in the nearby chapter house of the abbey of Westminster. If Henry had anything of particular importance to say he might well summon the Commons to appear before him – as he did in his first Parliament, in order to give them a lecture on his right to the throne. But strictly speaking the Commons took no part in Parliaments, except at the opening and closing ceremonies, when they squeezed into cramped positions at one end of the room (technically outside it) in which the King and Lords were seated, and made a report of their separate proceedings through the mouth of their Speaker.

The Speaker was elected by the Commons from among their own number, but in practice the election was a formality since the King had earlier indicated whom he wished to be chosen. All the Speakers of Henry's reign were royal nominees, selected from the knights of the shire who, as a group, had a certain pre-eminence in the Lower House. Two knights were elected for 37 out of the 39 English shires by freeholders who held land to the value of at least 40 shillings (£2) a year – the remaining two shires, Cheshire and County Durham, were as yet unenfranchised. The knights of the shire were outnumbered by the borough members – burgesses – who were elected on a variety of franchises. Not all burgesses were townsmen, however. The process had already started by which local landowners put themselves forward as candidates for election to a borough seat, often holding out the inducement of paying their own expenses if they were elected. It is possible that by 1500 as many as half the burgesses in the Lower House were in fact gentry.

Because they were linked with the High Court of Parliament, whose work must not be impeded by the processes of inferior courts, members of the Commons had certain privileges. They could not be arrested for debt, breach of contract, or other civil suit, while Parliament was in session. As for their discussions, if the Speaker mis-reported these, they had the right – formally granted to them, in response to the Speaker's request, at the opening of every Parliament

– to amend what he had said. From this limited privilege was to develop the great claim to freedom of speech, but no such claim was ever made by the Commons under Henry VII. Members stood in awe of the King and would be no more likely to criticise him inside the House than outside. While an individual MP might, on occasion, feel so strongly about a particular measure that he would openly oppose it, he risked incurring the royal wrath. This is the significance of the story told by Sir Thomas More's son-in-law that when More, who had been elected as a burgess to the 1504 Parliament, dared to oppose Henry's request for a grant of money (see above, p. 21) and

> made such arguments and reasons there against, that the King's demands were thereby overthrown ... one of the King's Privy Chamber, named Mr Tyler, being present thereat, brought word to the King out of the Parliament House, that a beardless boy had disappointed all his purposes. Whereupon the King, conceiving great indignation towards him, could not be satisfied until he had some way revenged it. And forasmuch as he, nothing having, nothing could lose, his grace devised a causeless quarrel against his father, keeping him in the Tower until he had paid him an hundred pounds fine. [13 *p.* 7]

Henry's success in controlling Parliament may be judged by the fact that although he amended a number of bills, he never needed to veto any. This was the result partly of careful management but mainly of the identity of interest between the King and the property-owners whom he summoned to meet him. Lancastrian Parliaments, and particularly the Commons, had pressed for the adoption of a reform programme that would make the royal household less wasteful and government more efficient. The property-owners now had a monarch who was putting that reform programme into effect, and they willingly co-operated with him. Only towards the end of Henry's reign did they begin to ask themselves whether they were paying too high a price.

THE FUNCTIONS OF PARLIAMENT

Parliaments were the occasion for a dialogue in which the King could learn about the state of the localities while the representatives of those localities could find out how proposed government measures would affect them. When members returned to their constituencies they were expected to act not simply as reporters, retailing the news from the capital, but also as government propagandists – since, by giving their consent in Parliament, they were committed even to unpopular measures like taxation. They could also be used in a more direct fashion, as in 1495 when they were given new standards of weights and measures to distribute in their localities.

While Parliament was useful as a means of two-way communication, it was essential for the granting of money (see above, pp. 18, 21). Yet if the institution's existence had depended solely upon its control over taxation, it would have ended after the first decade of Henry's reign, for by the late 1490s the King was not merely out of debt but beginning to accumulate a reserve of treasure. But Parliament had one other function which it alone could perform – namely, the making of statute law. While Henry had frequent recourse to royal proclamations to enforce his will, and considered them, in the words of R.W. Heinze, 'a useful and necessary instrument of governing . . . he never used them in a way that posed any threat to Parliament' [61 *p. 84*]. Statute was the highest form of law and, unlike proclamations, it was enforceable in common-law courts. Admittedly, the King appointed the judges who presided over these courts, and it was taken for granted that he should be consulted in cases which particularly concerned him before any decision was taken. Yet the King could not change the common law which the judges and courts administered unless he first obtained the consent of the Lords and Commons in Parliament.

Henry made considerable use of statute to carry out his policies. There were just under 200 public Acts passed during his reign, and the average number per parliamentary session was about the same as under Henry VIII. Many official measures made their first appearance in the Commons, for although members' principal concern was with private bills, which they put forward for the benefit of their particular constituencies, the House would draw up public bills on matters of general interest, and the promotion of these was often the work of royal Councillors sitting in the Commons. For this reason it is not always possible to distinguish between government proposals and those which genuinely originated out of the concerns of MPs.

One of the major functions of Parliament was the strengthening of the crown, and the first Parliament of Henry's reign declared, for the 'avoiding of all ambiguities and questions', that 'the inheritance of the crowns of the realms of England and of France . . . be, rest, remain and abide in the most royal person of our now sovereign lord King Harry the VIIth and in the heirs of his body lawfully coming'. There was no question, of course, of Henry seeking a 'parliamentary title' to the crown, which he claimed by right of descent. The object of the statute was simply to ensure that Henry's authority could not be challenged in the courts and that he should have full possession of all royal lands. The 'De Facto' Act of 1495 was another measure designed to strengthen Henry's hold on the throne by declaring that anyone giving 'true and faithful service' to the wearer of the crown should not subsequently be 'convict or attaint of high treason' for so doing.

As already mentioned (see above, p. 15), Parliament also reinforced Henry's position by crippling his enemies with Acts of attainder which transferred their property to the crown. These had been frequently used during the Wars of the Roses, and Henry followed suit by opening his reign with a batch of attainders against prominent Yorkists. His second Parliament saw 28 attainders, following the suppression of the Simnel conspiracy (see below, pp. 75–6), and Henry kept up this heavy pressure upon his opponents even after he had firmly established himself [*Doc. 14*]. His last Parliament, in 1504, passed more Acts of attainder than any of the others, and only the 1497 Parliament was entirely free of them.

Parliament was also useful in the campaign to restore order to a disturbed country, and over 10 per cent of the statutes passed during the reign dealt with the duties of Justices of the Peace. In 1485 an Act empowered them to issue a warrant for the arrest of any person and to carry out a preliminary examination on suspicion alone, without waiting for a formal indictment by a grand jury. And in 1495 came the Act authorising them to hear and determine, without indictment, all offences short of felony. They were also required by statute to supervise and control local officials and to amend jury panels chosen by the sheriff if the latter had failed to behave in an impartial manner.

Another sphere of parliamentary regulation concerned corporations and franchises, which were brought under closer royal control. Statutes were passed regulating the municipalities of Northampton and Leicester, and even the great metropolis of London was brought to heel. In 1487 an Act annulled City ordinances forbidding citizens to take their goods to fairs and markets outside the capital, and ten years later Parliament blocked the Merchant Adventurers' attempt to impose a prohibitively high entrance fee for membership of their company (see below, p. 67). This was followed by an Act of 1504 which laid down that 'no masters, wardens and fellowships of crafts ... nor any rulers of gilds or fraternities, take upon them to make any acts or ordinances' unless these were first 'examined and approved by the Chancellor, Treasurer of England, and Chief Justices of either Bench'. These statutes emphasised the principle that all jurisdictional and legislative rights derived from the crown and could, if the King saw good cause, be controlled or even resumed.

Parliamentary regulation was also applied to the economy. Acts prescribed licences for certain trades and laid down minimum standards of manufacture. These statutes were known as 'penal' because those found guilty of infringement were liable to a penalty. Half of this was to go to informers, who were thereby encouraged to act as unofficial government agents, and half to the King. Other Acts were designed to promote trade by improving the coinage and establishing uniform weights and measures. In 1485 and 1489 Navigation Acts were passed, designed to promote the shipping industry and through it the navy (see below, pp. 71–2).

Further measures were designed to limit the impact of economic changes and maintain social discipline. In 1489 came the first general Act against depopulation and eviction. It was followed by a statute of 1495 laying down maximum wage rates and minimum hours of work, and forbidding the withholding of labour. Another Act of that year ordered that vagabonds found in towns should be put in the stocks and then expelled; beggars were to be forcibly returned to their original place of residence.

Parliament's concern with the maintenance of order led it into the frontier land between Church and state, with the Act of 1489 limiting benefit of clergy (see below, p. 63). But it made no attempt in the reign of the first Tudor to invade the realm of spiritual matters. Although in many ways Parliament acted as a supreme lawgiver, it also acknowledged implicit boundaries upon its freedom of action. The big extension of parliamentary competence did not come until after 1529.

8   THE CHURCH

There were some 9,000 parishes in England, but at any one time a quarter of these were likely to be without a resident incumbent. This was not because of any shortage of clergy, for there may have been as many as 30,000 priests as well as hundreds of men in minor orders. Non-residence was usually the result of pluralism, for if a minister held more than one living he could clearly not be resident in all of them. The roots of pluralism went deep into the structure of the Church in England, for the *Ecclesia Anglicana* was the largest single organisation in the country and it needed a considerable bureaucracy to enable it to function. Clerical bureaucrats were therefore appointed to one or more parishes on the understanding that while they would draw the tithes, they would not be resident or perform any pastoral functions. These would be carried out instead by a curate, to whom they would pay a small stipend [28].

This system was not without its merits. It was better for the Church to be run by clerics rather than lay administrators, and there was no reason why a curate should not be as committed or effective as an incumbent. But as the historian of the diocese of Lincoln has pointed out, there was another side to the picture:

> From the point of view of the parish, tithe paid to a non-resident was so much money down the drain. The curate or priest in charge of livings which supported non-resident incumbents would have felt much the same way. Few of them received more than £5 for doing all the work of the parish; they were often paid less than a quarter of the real value of the living. [107 *p. 103*].

It was generally reckoned that an income of £15 a year was sufficient for a parish priest to fulfil his obligations without being overburdened with financial worries, but only about one in four parishes produced as much as this. In half, the income of the incumbent was under £10. It would have made economic sense to amalgamate the poorer livings, but in practice it was often the richer ones which were subject to pluralism, since this was the easiest way of providing an adequate income for a clerical bureaucrat. The irony of the situation was that the Church had succeeded in raising the educational level of its clergy, but had not thereby benefited the parishes. University-trained clerics, usually with a degree in civil or canon law, were all too frequently snapped up either by bishops, who needed them for diocesan administration, or by the crown, which was largely dependent upon clerics, from bishops downwards, for running the state [109].

Non-residence and pluralism helped perpetuate the division of the clergy into a highly paid minority and a clerical proletariat. Among the most highly paid were the bishops. Eleven English sees were worth over £1,000 a year, and a few of them a great deal more – the Bishop of Winchester, for instance, could count on a minimum of £3,500. All bishops were appointed, in effect, by the King, for papal confirmation was a mere formality. Elevation to the episcopate was usually a reward for service to the crown, and Henry, unlike his Lancastrian predecessors, chose men on merit rather than birth: only three of his bishops came from noble families. He preferred lawyers to theologians, and of 33 bishops appointed by him, fifteen had degrees in law, compared with eight in theology. A number of bishops had degrees in canon law – the law of the Church – but Henry showed a preference for ecclesiastics who were experts in civil or Roman law. Cardinal John Morton, for instance, whom Henry selected as Archbishop of Canterbury, was a Doctor of Civil Law and had practised in the ecclesiastical Court of Arches.

Morton was an autocrat by temperament and conservative in outlook. Yet he was devoted to the interests of the Church and determined to improve its effectiveness within the existing limits [28; 112]. Much the same was true of his fellow bishops, though their role as civil servants left them little time for ecclesiastical matters. Richard Fox, for example, began Henry's reign as Bishop of Exeter and was translated from there to Wells, but his official duties as Lord Privy Seal and one of Henry's leading Councillors were so heavy that he never found time to set foot in either cathedral. The consciousness of this neglect of his spiritual functions weighed heavily upon him, and towards the end of his life he was glad to abandon the service of the state and devote himself to the see of Winchester, of which he was by then bishop. He also founded Corpus Christi College at Oxford and showed his interest in the new learning of the Renaissance by making provision for lectures in Greek as well as Latin. Another patron of learning was John Fisher, whom Henry appointed Bishop of Rochester in 1504. Fisher was confessor to Henry's mother, Lady Margaret Beaufort, a deeply devout woman who saw the need to strengthen the Christian faith through education. It was at Fisher's suggestion that she instituted the Lady Margaret chairs in divinity at both universities and provided the money for building Christ's College at Cambridge [26; 28; 119].

Despite the fact that an increasing proportion of clergy had received a university education, there is little indication that they had been affected by the new learning. Many priests possessed books, but they were mainly traditional works of piety, and surprisingly enough they rarely included the Bible. One reason for this may have been the lack of any official translation: unofficial ones were associated with the Lollards (see below) and therefore tainted with heresy. Books of hours, service books and lives of the saints were the usual fare, not only for clergy but also for the literate lay reader, and they were turned out in large numbers by the printing press established at Westminster by John Caxton and taken over after his death in 1491 by his assistant, Wynkyn de Worde [107; 109; 113.]

While the *Ecclesia Anglicana* was firmly established and apparently popular, it was not without its critics. Among the most threatening had been the Lollards, who believed that the Church must be purified by being stripped of its wealth. The Lollards had gone beyond criticism into heresy by denying transubstantiation and refusing to accept any doctrine which could not be justified from the Bible, which they translated into the vernacular. Savage repression in the early fifteenth century had driven Lollardy underground, and for a time it seemed to have disappeared. However, the restoration of strong government enabled the ecclesiastical authorities to renew their investigations, and they soon discovered evidence of continuing Lollard activity. Over 70 prosecutions for heresy have been recorded for Henry VII's reign. In the great majority of cases the heretics confessed and repented and were only required to do public penance; the handful who remained obdurate were burnt at the stake [Doc. 16]. Among these was a priest whom Henry himself convinced of his errors while he was actually tied to the stake; he did not, however, escape the flames [20].

Henry was entirely orthodox in religion [Doc. 20], which was just as well, since he needed the support of the Pope for his fledgling dynasty. He had taken care, when in exile, to assure the papacy of his commitment to it, and this paid off in the opening years of his reign, when Innocent VIII signalled his approval of the new ruler. So conscious was Henry of the need to conserve good relations with Rome that in 1492 he asked one of the cardinals resident there to act on his behalf in all matters affecting England. This appointment of a Cardinal Protector was the first to be made by any sovereign and helped ensure a favourable response to the various requests which Henry made [120]. He had no difficulty in securing papal confirmation of his nominations to the episcopal bench, and he also obtained approval for restrictions upon the traditional rights of sanctuary and benefit of clergy. Sanctuaries were prescribed areas, usually in or around an ecclesiastical building, in which criminals could take refuge and be free from arrest. Henry was determined that this privilege should not apply to traitors, and in 1487 a judicial decision to this effect was confirmed by a papal bull which withdrew the privilege from anyone who used it to commit further offences, and allowed the King to station guards outside sanctuaries harbouring dangerous criminals [114].

Benefit of clergy was the name given to the practice whereby offenders claiming to be in holy orders could demonstrate their clerical status by reading through a 'neck verse', whereupon they would be handed over for punishment to the ecclesiastical authorities instead of being dealt with (more harshly) by the common-law courts. This privilege had become widely abused, since it extended to those in minor orders, who were clergy only in name, and even to barely literate laymen. In 1489, therefore, Parliament passed an Act limiting benefit of clergy, except for the first offence, to those who provided proof that they really were in holy orders.

The Church would have been well advised to abolish minor orders, but it did not do so. Its conservatism, amounting at times to lethargy, prompted a number of individuals to take the lead in pressing for an attack upon abuses. Prominent among these was John Colet, who was famous for his Oxford lectures on the New Testament, and whose associates included William Grocyn, a pioneer of Greek studies in England, Thomas Linacre, a distinguished physician and classicist, and young Thomas More. Erasmus, who came to England for the first time in 1499, was delighted to find such a circle of humanists awaiting him, and declared that when he heard Colet speak he felt he was listening to Plato. Colet and his friends were not without supporters among the bishops, principally Richard Fox, John Fisher and William Warham.

Henry himself was well disposed towards them, as he demonstrated by appointing Colet as Dean of St Paul's in 1504 and subsequently announcing his intention (never, alas, fulfilled) to provide a benefice for Erasmus.

Henry's particular concern was with the religious orders, and as early as 1487 he petitioned the Pope for assistance in regenerating them. Innocent VIII responded with a bull empowering Archbishop Morton to visit and reform all religious houses, including those which were technically exempt from royal authority. Henry set an example by taking under his protection the community of Franciscan Observants established at Greenwich by Edward IV. The Observants, unlike the Conventuals, adhered to the pattern of life and worship originally prescribed by St Francis, and Henry showed his approval of their austere spirituality not simply by transferring to the Observants the three Conventual houses at Canterbury, Newcastle and Southampton, but also by establishing, in 1501, a new Observant foundation in the grounds of his palace at Richmond in Surrey [108]. In his will, Henry left several hundred pounds apiece to the Observant houses, partly as an expression of 'our long continued devotion towards St Francis, their patron', but also because 'we always have had a special confidence and trust in the devout prayers of the Friars Observants of this our royaume' [16 *pp. 30–1*].

The overall picture of the *Ecclesia Anglicana* in Henry VII's reign is that of an institution which, despite its obvious flaws, commanded the allegiance of the great majority of English people, from the King downwards. Evidence of this survives to the present day, for Henry's munificence in adding to Westminster Abbey the resplendent chapel which bears his name was matched by corporations, gilds, and ordinary men and women throughout the land. The late fifteenth and early sixteenth centuries saw the rebuilding and beautifying of hundreds of parish churches, and the fact that people were prepared to spend their money in this way is evidence that the Church was a valued and integral part of English society.

9 THE ECONOMY

The economy of England in Henry VII's reign was based upon agriculture, most of which was for subsistence, and its health fluctuated with the quality of the harvests. The early 1480s had been bad years, but in 1485, the year of Henry's accession, the harvest was good, and this upturn was maintained right through the 1490s. Good harvests undoubtedly promoted social stability and helped Henry in the task of establishing his new dynasty. But his luck ran out in the closing decade of his reign, and there were four bad harvests in a row between 1500 and 1503 – a period of dearth which accounts for the concern with public order shown in the Parliament of 1504 [130].

Apart from food, the most important single commodity was wool, which formed the basis of England's major industry and accounted, indirectly, for some 90 per cent of English exports. The demand for wool had a marked effect upon the pattern of English farming, since many landowners found it more profitable to turn their estates over to sheep than to continue cultivating them in the traditional manner. This affected the rural community in three main ways, through enclosure, engrossing (the amalgamation of holdings under single ownership), and depopulation – an unholy trinity which came to be the bugbear of Tudor governments.

Enclosure meant, strictly speaking, the fencing-off of a man's property and the extinguishing of common rights over it, so that it could be cultivated without reference to the community. The advantage of enclosure was that it enabled the progressive farmer to develop his own techniques without being held back by the incompetence, conservatism or laziness of his neighbours. But it had adverse effects when it involved the eviction of families. Freeholders could claim a share of the land to be enclosed; copyholders, who held a copy of the entry in the manorial court roll as evidence of their tenure, also had a right to compensation which could be enforced in Chancery and the prerogative courts if the common-law courts (which were, in fact, beginning to take cognisance of copyholds during Henry's reign) refused to act. But tenants-at-will, cottagers and squatters had no legal tenure and, if they were evicted, no resources and nowhere to go.

Enclosure – using this term, as contemporaries did, to include engrossing – was a frequent cause of riots in Henry's reign. At Coventry, for instance, in 1496, the rich burgesses of the town council decided to enclose the Lammas fields on which many of the inhabitants grazed their sheep and cattle. The opposition to this move was led by one of the townsmen, who distributed propaganda verses such as those which started

The city is bond that should be free.
The right is holden from the commonalty.
Our commons, that at Lammas open should be cast,
They be closed in and hedged full fast. [14, III *p. 13*]

As far as the destruction of villages was concerned, most of the damage had been done before Henry VII came to the throne, but his government was sufficiently alarmed to pass the first legislation against the practice. An Act of 1489 was specifically directed to the Isle of Wight which, because of conversion of arable to pasture and engrossing, was said to be 'desolate and not inhabited, but occupied with beasts and cattle'. The same year also saw a general Act which recited how 'great inconveniencies daily doth increase by desolation and pulling-down and wilful waste of houses and towns within this .\.. realm, and laying to pasture lands which customably have been used in tilth', and complained that 'where in some towns two hundred persons were occupied and lived by their lawful labours, now be there occupied two or three herdsmen'. However, the only remedy provided by the Act was an order that all towns and houses should in future be maintained and not allowed to decay – a pious hope, but not very effective in halting the economic forces that were transforming the countryside.

Although Henry VII's government, like that of his successors, was formally opposed to depopulating enclosures, some of the chief offenders were themselves in royal service. At Wormleighton, for instance, on the borders of Warwickshire and Northamptonshire, William Cope, Cofferer of the Household, evicted the inhabitants of fifteen tenements in October 1498, enclosed 240 acres of arable with hedges and ditches, and turned the newly created field over to sheep. Sixty persons lost their dwellings as a result of this operation and were forced to depart 'tearfully' [122; 123]. Another of Henry's officers who was accused of depopulating enclosures was Edward Belknap (see above, p. 18). Yet it should be added that in both these cases, and perhaps in many others in the Midland region of England, the villages which were destroyed had long been declining. In such places enclosure was the virtually inevitable conclusion to a process of decay that had been taking place over many decades [125; 128].

WOOL AND CLOTH

The obverse of this gloomy picture is the prosperity of the trade in wool and woollen cloth, and of the towns and villages – mainly in the Midlands and East Anglia – which thrived on it. The clothier was a familiar figure in Henry VII's England, riding round the country buying wool and arranging for its collection and distribution to centres where it could either be packed for export or else woven into cloth. Export of raw wool had been declining because of the heavy taxation imposed on it, as well as the growing demand of the native cloth industry. This decline continued throughout Henry's reign, and by 1509 wool exports were some 30 per cent lower than they had been in 1485. This affected the Merchants of the Staple, who had a monopoly of the export of raw wool to Calais, the staple town, and were financially responsible for the maintenance of the garrison there. But while the trade in raw wool was shrinking, the export of cloth was expanding, and 60 per cent more cloth was being sent abroad by the end of Henry's reign than had been exported in the early years.

The leading part in the export of cloth was taken by the Merchant Adventurers of London, who dominated the trade with Antwerp. However, their attempts to establish a monopoly of cloth exports led to friction with merchants from 'outports' such as Bristol and Boston. The London company took the first step towards establishing a monopoly in 1496, when it declared that anyone trading in cloth should pay it the prohibitively high fee of £20. This unilateral action brought the Adventurers up against Parliament, where the Londoners were in a minority, and an Act of the following year, condemning 'their uncharitable and inordinate covetousness', ordered them to reduce their fee by two-thirds.

While Henry was willing to restrain the Merchant Adventurers at home for fear that they would constrict trade instead of expanding it, he gave them full support abroad. In 1505 a royal charter authorised the company to inspect cloth and maintain standards of quality, and also to settle disputes and take whatever other measures it thought necessary for the efficient functioning of the trade. The Adventurers' entrance fee was now fixed at £5 – the implication being that they could have a virtual monopoly of cloth exports on condition that they did not attempt to confine membership to an oligarchy of rich merchants.

The main outlet for the sale of English cloth was Antwerp, which was rapidly becoming the commercial capital of Europe. Yet while English merchants valued Antwerp for its convenience, they were not dependent upon it. Cloth was so essential a commodity that buyers would follow wherever the market moved. The factories of Flanders, on the other hand, which specialised in refining the coarse English cloth and turning it into a variety of fabrics, were firmly fixed, and this gave Henry a weapon he did not hesitate to use. In 1493, when the ruler of the Netherlands was giving support to the pretender, Perkin Warbeck, Henry ordered the Adventurers to move to Calais, and his embargo on trade with the Netherlands remained in force until 1496. The Netherlands retaliated with a counter-embargo on English goods, and although trade between the two countries did not completely dry up, it was irregular and restricted. A return to sanity was signalled by the signing of the *Magnus Intercursus* in 1496. Under the terms of this agreement English merchants were free to sell their goods wholesale anywhere in the Duke of Burgundy's dominions except Flanders itself, and were guaranteed swift and fair justice, a regular machinery for the settlement of disputes, and immunity from new tolls or duties.

The *Magnus Intercursus* did not, in practice, put an end to disputes between the Merchant Adventurers and the government of the Netherlands. However, Henry found his bargaining power unexpectedly strengthened when gales drove Philip, Duke of Burgundy, into an English port in 1506. Philip now became the guest of Henry, who persuaded him to agree to a commercial treaty giving English merchants unprecedented privileges. The name given by Bacon to this agreement – *Malus Intercursus* – is accurate enough, since it was certain to cause so much offence in the Netherlands that it would be inoperative. This was indeed the case, and in 1507 the *status quo* was restored by mutual agreement.

THE EXPANSION OF OVERSEAS TRADE

Trade between England and France, based principally on wine from Gascony and woad from Toulouse, had been hampered by French restrictions during the Yorkist period. In 1486 Henry VII signed a commercial agreement with France which led to their removal, but the French king reimposed them as a consequence of the quarrel over Brittany (see below, pp. 76–81). Not until 1495 were they entirely swept away – part of the price that France had to pay for English neutrality during the Italian wars – and in 1497 a new treaty confirmed the privileges of English merchants trading with the King of France's dominions.

In 1489 Henry renewed the treaty of friendship with Portugal that had been concluded over a hundred years earlier. He also took steps to expand the role of English merchants in trade with Spain. By the commercial clauses of the 1489 Treaty of Medina del Campo, English and Spanish merchants were given reciprocal privileges and low duties in each other's countries. English merchants' share of trade with Spain increased significantly as a consequence of the Navigation Acts (see below, p. 71), but Spain retaliated with similar measures. Now that trade in one direction was confined to Spanish ships, and in the other to English ones, expansion was brought to a halt. Even so, by the end of the reign English merchants had a larger share in trade between the two countries than had been the case at Henry's accession.

Since the middle of the fifteenth century English merchants had been pushing into the eastern Mediterranean, buying wines from Crete and currants from the Levant. This brought them up against the Venetians who, alarmed at this threat to their commercial supremacy, imposed heavy duties upon the export of wines from their territories. Henry reacted, in 1490, by making a treaty with Florence, one of Venice's rivals, whereby the Florentine port of Pisa became a staple for English wool. Two years later he took more direct action by imposing a heavy duty upon wine brought to England in Venetian ships. This tit-for-tat policy might have continued indefinitely but for the outbreak of the Italian wars. The formation of the League of Cambrai (see below, p. 86) threatened the very existence of Venice, and she had neither the time nor the energy for a peripheral commercial quarrel. By the time Henry died, therefore, English merchants had built up a flourishing trade with Pisa and the Levant [135].

The challenge to Venice was one of the reasons which led Henry to patronise those explorers who believed that a route to the east, with its fabulous silks and spices, could be found by sailing west, thereby outflanking the Venetian domination of the established trade routes. Henry narrowly missed becoming the patron of Columbus, but in 1496 he issued letters patent to John Cabot – ironically enough a Venetian by origin – authorising him 'to sail to all parts, regions and coasts of the eastern, western and northern sea'. When Cabot returned from his first voyage of 1497, during which he discovered Newfoundland, Henry gave him audience, listened attentively to his account of his adventures, and encouraged him to set out again the following year. Cabot never returned from this second voyage, but Henry extended royal patronage to his son, Sebastian, authorising him to settle any territories which were not already occupied by Christian states. In 1506 the Bristol company of 'Adventurers in the New Found Lands' was formed, and this backed Sebastian Cabot's next voyage, in which he probably explored Hudson Bay and the North American coast. By the time he returned home, however, Henry VII was dead, and with him any hope that England might join Spain and Portugal among the pioneers of exploration and settlement in the New World.

In his dealings with France, Venice, and to a lesser extent Spain, Henry was reasonably successful. Further north, however, he had to reckon with the mighty Hanseatic League of German cities, which had its headquarters at Lübeck. The Hansards had provided the ships which helped Edward IV regain his throne. In return, by the 1474 Treaty of Utrecht, he had granted them partial exemption from taxation and the right to import goods at a lower rate of duty than that paid by native English merchants. At their London base in the Steelyard, and in Southampton and Boston, the Hansards had set up depots which were virtually independent states.

Henry VII's attitude towards the Hanse was ambiguous. In 1486 he confirmed their privileges as defined in the Treaty of Utrecht, but he permitted the passage of the Navigation Acts of 1485 and 1489 which implied a threat to the Hanse's control of the carrying trade with northern Europe. This was not the only legislation aimed at the League. An Act of 1487 prohibited the export of unfinished cloth by alien merchants, and two years later the Hanse was denied the right to take bullion out of England. In 1504, on the other hand, Henry sponsored an Act declaring the Hanse's privileges to be sacrosanct, but this was at a time when he feared that the League might support the Yorkist pretender, the Earl of Suffolk, who had sought refuge in Germany (see below, p. 83) [141].

Even if Henry was wary of antagonising the powerful League, particularly at moments of crisis, he could not ignore pressure from his own merchants. Complaints that the Hanse was financing the Dutch privateers which preyed on English shipping led Henry, in 1489, to issue letters of marque and reprisal, and there was a danger that the dispute would escalate into open war between England and the Hanse. Attempts at a negotiated settlement in May 1491 ended in failure, and Henry seems to have condoned anti-Hanse actions. In 1493, when a London mob attacked the Steelyard, Henry paid only minimal compensation. He subsequently demanded £20,000 from the League as security that they would not break his embargo on trade with the Netherlands, and in 1508 he confiscated this sum on the grounds that they had done so. He also limited the Hansards' right to import goods at low rates of duty to those items which originated in Hanse towns and territories [141].

In 1489–90 an agreement with Denmark gave English merchants freedom to trade in Denmark and Norway as well as the right to fish in Icelandic waters. This was a step towards Henry's long-term objective of obtaining direct access for his subjects to the valuable Baltic market, where they could exchange their highly prized cloth for naval stores and corn. But his success was limited, for the Hanse was too rich and powerful to be easily overthrown, and English shipping had not yet developed to the point where it could take full advantage of the gains made by Henry's diplomacy.

THE ENCOURAGEMENT OF ENGLISH SHIPPING

English shipping at the beginning of Henry's reign was caught up in a vicious circle. While Hansard ships were available, there was little incentive for the building of English ones; yet the lack of English ships meant there was no possibility of mounting an effective challenge to the Hanse. Those members of the Commons with commercial interests were well aware of the need to build up England's maritime and naval strength, and it was probably pressure from them that led to the passing of the Navigation Acts of 1485 and 1489. The first Act, calling to mind 'the great [di]minishing and decay that hath been now of late time of the navy within this realm of England, and idleness of the mariners within the same, by the which this noble realm, within short process of time, without reformation be had therein, shall not be of ability and power to defend itself', ordered that in future wines from Guienne and Gascony should be imported only in English ships with a predominantly English crew [*Doc. 17*]. The 1489 Act added a general provision that English merchants should not import any goods in foreign ships when English ones were available. The outcry of the Hansards, as well as the Spanish decision to pass similar legislation, suggest that this early exercise in mercantilism was relatively successful.

The connection between merchant shipping and naval defence was very close, since merchant vessels often became warships in times of crisis. Edward IV had created a royal navy, and Richard III maintained a fleet of some ten ships. Henry VII showed less commitment, and by the end of his reign there were only five 'King's ships'. But he improved the facilities available for this small fleet by constructing at Portsmouth the first known dry dock in Europe [133]. He also encouraged the development of the iron and gunfounding industries. In 1491 he authorised the establishment of an ironworks in Ashdown forest in the Sussex Weald, where wood and ore were to be found in abundance, and he persuaded foreign craftsmen to settle in England, where they could instruct his subjects in the latest techniques of gunfounding [121].

The creation of a dry dock at Portsmouth was the inspiration of the ubiquitous Sir Reginald Bray, who had earlier supervised the construction at Southampton of the 450-ton *Sovereign*, which carried 141 guns. Meanwhile, Bray's fellow-Councillor, Sir Richard Guildford, had been directing the building of the *Regent* – an even larger ship of 600 tons and 225 guns. These 'great ships', as they were appropriately called, were very expensive to build – the *Regent* cost close on £1,000 – so it is hardly surprising that Henry encouraged his subjects to share the burden. He offered tax concessions to merchants who built new ships, with a special bounty for vessels larger than 70 tons [133]. Despite these initiatives, however, the English merchant marine remained inadequate, at least in the short term. When Henry invaded France in 1492, more than half of the ships needed to transport his army had to be hired from the Flemings [132].

One reason for Henry's interest in English shipping was his personal involvement in commercial affairs. As well as hiring out royal ships to English merchants, he engaged in the alum trade and in 1505–6 made £15,000 from the import of this essential ingredient for the manufacture of soap. Henry was also concerned to increase his income from Customs duties. He made interest-free loans to merchants on condition that their trade benefited the Customs by a stipulated amount and in 1507 he introduced a new Book of Rates, listing the amount of duty on specific items. The yield from Customs would inevitably have risen as stable conditions were restored, but the increase of over 20 per cent, from about £33,000 in 1485 to over £40,000 by 1509, suggests that Henry's intervention bore fruit.

The overall impact of Henry's policies on English trade is difficult to estimate. In northern Europe his success was limited; in southern Europe it was greater. But there was little change in the pattern of trade between England and the Netherlands, which was the major artery of English commerce. English merchants were responsible for only a little over half this trade. The Hanse had a quarter and other alien merchants the remainder. All one can say with respect to these figures is that without Henry's encouragement the role of English merchants might have been even smaller. The long-term effect of his policy was perhaps more important, for he sketched out the lines – into the Baltic and the Mediterranean, and across the Atlantic – along which English commerce was eventually to develop.

10 FOREIGN POLICY

THE STATES OF WESTERN EUROPE

Western Europe during Henry VII's reign was dominated by two great states, France and Spain, and to a lesser extent by the Holy Roman Empire, which encompassed modern-day Germany and parts of what is now eastern France.

The general tenor of French policy was to extend the kingdom to its 'natural' boundaries, although this aim was never consistently or consciously pursued, and France gained its greatest triumphs as much by accident as by design. Louis XI had been particularly successful, and by the time he died, in 1483, had nearly doubled the amount of territory held by the French crown. He left as his heir the thirteen-year-old Charles VIII.

Spain had been united only in 1479, ten years after the marriage of Ferdinand, King of Aragon, to Isabella, Queen of Castile. The southern part of the peninsula was still, however, occupied by the Moors, and Ferdinand and Isabella, 'the Catholic Monarchs', made it their lives' work to drive them out. In this they were successful, and in January 1492, just before Columbus set off on a journey that would give them a whole new world to rule, they completed the conquest of the last Moorish kingdom, Granada.

Ten years before Henry VII came to the throne of England it looked as if a third power, Burgundy, would develop into a major state. However, in 1477 its great duke, Charles the Bold, died and his territories were divided. Large parts of Burgundy were seized by France, but the Netherlands, including Flanders, went to Charles's daughter Mary, who in 1477 married the young Habsburg Archduke, Maximilian of Austria. In 1493, following the death of his father, the Emperor Frederick III, Maximilian was elected to the imperial throne, and since by this time Mary was dead, the government of the Netherlands devolved upon their son, Philip, Duke of Burgundy.

BURGUNDY, IRELAND AND LAMBERT SIMNEL, 1485-87

The reaction of the Archduke Maximilian, the virtual ruler of Burgundy, to the news of Henry Tudor's accession to the English throne was one of alarm. Burgundy had enjoyed good relations with the Yorkists – as shown by the marriage of Charles the Bold to Edward IV's sister, Margaret – but the new Tudor King owed his crown to the support of France, which was Burgundy's enemy. Maximilian made a bid for Henry's friendship by sending heralds to congratulate him upon his accession, but the King did not respond. This may have been simply an oversight on Henry's part. He was, after all, an inexperienced ruler, preoccupied with establishing his position at home. But it is equally possible that his neglect of the customary courtesies was deliberate. Having spent part of his exile in France, he could well have absorbed the French distrust of Burgundy. He must also have been aware that Maximilian had a better claim than his own to the English throne, being directly descended, through the female line, from Edward III's third surviving son, John of Gaunt (see Genealogy, p. 114).

Henry made matters worse by his treatment of Charles the Bold's widow, Margaret of Burgundy, which turned her into one of his most committed enemies. Edward IV had granted his sister a number of lucrative trading licences, but at the beginning of Henry VII's reign these privileges were withdrawn. It is hardly surprising that the embittered Duchess subsequently gave her support and encouragement to Yorkist pretenders to Henry's throne. In this initial foray into the minefield of European diplomacy Henry had shown a distinct lack of finesse [142].

The first pretender to make his challenge known was Lambert Simnel, the ten-year-old son of an organ-builder. He was the pupil of an Oxford priest named Richard Simonds, who noticed a marked resemblance between Simnel and Edward IV's nephew, the young Earl of Warwick, who had been a prisoner in the Tower since the beginning of Henry's reign. In 1486 Simonds took Simnel to Ireland, where Yorkist support was strong, and won recognition for him from the Irish nobles, led by the Lord Deputy, the Earl of Kildare. When Henry heard of this, he attempted to undermine Simnel's credibility by parading the real Earl of Warwick through the streets of London, but the conspirators declared that Warwick was the imposter, not Simnel. Henry's problems became more acute when the Earl of Lincoln, the nephew and chosen successor of Richard III, fled to Flanders, where he joined the Yorkist peer, Viscount Lovell.

There they won the support of Margaret of Burgundy, who provided them with a force of 2,000 German *landsknechts*, or mercenaries, to assist Simnel, whom she acknowledged as her nephew. Her action was almost certainly sanctioned by Maximilian, for the *landsknechts* were led by Martin Schwartz, who had earlier served as one of his captains.

The expeditionary force arrived in Ireland on 5 May 1487, and on 24 May, Whitsunday, Lambert was solemnly crowned in Dublin Cathedral as Edward VI, with the aid of a gold circlet borrowed from a statue of the Virgin Mary. Early in June, Simnel and his army – increased in numbers if not in strength by poorly armed Irish levies – landed on the coast of Lancashire, hoping to win support in the north of England, where Richard III had been well respected and even loved. They were to be disappointed, however, for only a handful of dissidents came in to join them. The rebel army, numbering some 8,000 men, now turned south-east, and by 16 June 1487 it had reached East Stoke, not far from Newark in Nottinghamshire. There its way was blocked by a 12,000-strong royal army under Henry's personal command. In a battle lasting three hours, the rebels were utterly routed. Lincoln, Schwartz and Thomas Geraldine, the leader of the Irish contingent, were all killed, with nearly half their men. Lovell escaped and fled to Scotland. As for the self-styled 'Edward VI', he was taken prisoner and began a new, but less glamorous, career as a turnspit in the royal kitchens.

THE BRETON CRISIS, 1487–92

The Simnel crisis was a direct consequence of Henry's failure to mend his bridges with Burgundy, and it is hardly surprising that once the danger was over he opened negotiations with Maximilian. These concluded in January 1488 with the signing of treaties which restored friendly relations and close commercial ties. Henry needed Maximilian's support because a new crisis was developing, concerning the future of Brittany. This independent duchy was ruled over by the aged Duke Francis II, who had no male heir. Anne of Beaujeu, who governed France in the name of her young brother, Charles VIII, hoped to incorporate Brittany into the French crown, but Francis countered this by offering the hand of his daughter, Anne of Brittany, to Maximilian. Unfortunately for Francis, he did not have the full support of the Breton nobles, a number of whom appealed to Anne of Beaujeu to intervene. She responded in May 1487 by sending French troops into the Duchy.

Henry was alarmed by this development, for the Breton ports offered convenient springboards for an invasion of England, and he feared for his own security if they were to come under French control. On the other hand, he had spent the last part of his exile as a guest at the French court and had been dependent upon French assistance for his own successful invasion of England. Gratitude pulled him in one direction, while strategic considerations pushed him in another. Henry appeared to vacillate, but in fact the strength and effectiveness of Breton resistance to the French invasion gave him time to weigh his options. The Breton army had been fortified by the arrival of foreign volunteers, including 1,500 sent by Maximilian, 1,000 from the rulers of Spain, Ferdinand and Isabella, and over 4,000 from Alain d'Albret, a French nobleman who, like Maximilian, hoped to acquire Brittany for himself by marrying its heiress. Several hundred Englishmen under Lord Scales also helped to swell the Breton ranks. Henry formally forbade Scales to intervene in the conflict, but made no attempt to stop him going to Brittany. A public disavowal of this sort enabled Henry to preserve good relations with France [138]. Indeed, in May 1488 he sent his almoner, Christopher Urswick, to the French court to try to negotiate a settlement, under which Anne of Brittany would be married off to Henry's ward, the young Duke of Buckingham [18].

As long as the Bretons continued to oppose the French takeover, Henry could afford to remain neutral. However, in July 1488 the situation was transformed by the crushing defeat of the Breton army at St Aubin du Cormier. Francis had to accept the terms of the Treaty of Sablé, including the provision that his daughter should not marry without French consent. Not only did this block the proposed marriage between Anne of Brittany and Maximilian, it also opened the way, as Anne of Beaujeu intended, to a marriage between Anne and Charles VIII which would lead to the incorporation of Brittany into France. This prospect became imminent only three weeks after the signing of the peace treaty, when Duke Francis died, and the twelve-year-old Anne became Duchess of Brittany in her own right. France claimed custody of the new ruler, but the Breton nobles, fearful for their independence, opposed the demand. A renewal of the fighting became inevitable, and this time Henry would not be able to stand aloof [138].

In order to make sure of his support at home, Henry summoned a Great Council in November 1488 (see above, p. 52). No record of its deliberations has survived, but it seems likely that it provided Henry with the encouragement he was seeking [105]. This was given tangible expression three months later, when Parliament voted £100,000 for raising and maintaining an army of 10,000 men. Having gained the backing of English public opinion, Henry was now free to enlist foreign allies. First came the Treaty of Dordrecht with Burgundy, in February 1489, to be followed, a month later, by the Treaty of Medina del Campo with Spain.

Although Henry had found allies, they were unable to give him immediate support. The principal Burgundian cities disapproved of Maximilian's anti-French policy, since this meant they were heavily taxed at the same time as they were deprived of valuable trade. Early in 1488 Maximilian established his residence at Bruges, hoping to overawe the citizens, but they closed the gates and held him prisoner inside. He only secured his release by agreeing to give up his regency and allow the towns, in effect, to decide on policy. No sooner was Maximilian free than he denounced these terms and took up the struggle once again. The towns appealed to France for help, and Charles VIII, anxious to prevent Maximilian from becoming involved in Brittany, readily agreed to be their 'Protector' [138].

Viewed in the context of the Breton crisis, the Treaty of Medina del Campo with Spain was equally disappointing. Ferdinand had insisted that Henry should bind himself not to make a separate peace, yet reserved the right to withdraw from the conflict if France restored Cerdagne and Roussillon, which adjoined Spain's north-west frontier. Furthermore, England was to commit herself to war with France immediately, while Spain could wait until the following year. It is sometimes assumed that Henry was duped by Ferdinand into accepting a treaty which had nothing to offer him, but this is not really the case. In dynastic terms Henry benefited greatly, for Ferdinand and Isabella not only bound themselves to bar Yorkist pretenders from Spanish soil, they also agreed to a marriage between their daughter, Catherine, and Henry's eldest son, Prince Arthur. Medina del Campo, then, marked the acceptance of the Tudor dynasty by one of the greatest powers in Europe, and it is probably no coincidence that Henry chose this moment to issue a new coin, the golden sovereign, on which he was displayed wearing not the traditional open crown of Kings of England but an imperial crown, closed over the head with hoops. It was a clear statement of Henry's belief that he was now the equal of any ruler in Christendom [46].

Despite the fact that he had failed to secure promises of immediate assistance from his allies, Henry committed himself to the support of Brittany, but only at minimum expense. Under the terms of the Treaty of Redon of February 1489, the Duchess Anne promised to cover the costs of an English expeditionary force, and to hand over Morlaix and Concarneau as sureties. Henry thereupon despatched 3,000 well-equipped troops to Brittany. At the same time he honoured his obligations under the Treaty of Dordrecht by ordering another force of 3,000 men to march from Calais to Dixmunde, where a garrison loyal to Maximilian was under siege from Flemish rebels and their French allies. This operation was successful and Dixmunde was relieved, but Maximilian did not, as Henry had hoped, join in the campaign to save Brittany. Maximilian's principal concern was now to assist his father, the Emperor Frederick III, in the conquest of Hungary, and in order to do this he needed to secure his Burgundian flank. In July 1489, therefore, he signed the Treaty of Frankfurt with France, by which he agreed not to intervene in Brittany, in return for a French promise not to aid the Flemish rebels against him. As a result of Maximilian's *volte face*, Spain's rulers, sensing that their chance of recovering Cerdagne and Roussillon by force was fast slipping away, offered Charles VIII the hand of a Spanish infanta in return for their abandonment of Brittany. These blows to Henry's hopes were followed by even worse news, for in October 1489 the Breton army was defeated and Anne had to accept terms which required her to dismiss the English troops in her service [138].

By the end of 1489 Henry's carefully laid plans to save Brittany lay in tatters. However, he refused to accept defeat, and instead of withdrawing his troops he despatched a further 3,000 in February 1490. In September of that year he at last persuaded Maximilian to rejoin the fray, but the Archduke exacted a significant price; in December he secretly married Duchess Anne. He did so not in person but by proxy, which cast doubts on the marriage's validity. The French responded by sending a powerful army to attack Rennes, the Breton capital, at a time when the mercenaries in Breton service were mutinous for lack of pay. In May 1491 Anne and Maximilian appealed to Henry for further aid, and he duly summoned another Great Council, which authorised the collection of a Benevolence. Subsequently, he obtained a parliamentary grant of two Fifteenths and Tenths for the prosecution of the war. Finally, in November 1491, he negotiated an accord which committed Spain to renew the struggle against France, though not until June 1492. This delay was realistic, in view of the fact that the money grants voted to Henry would take time to convert into soldiers and munitions, but it was too long for the Bretons. In December 1491, Anne bowed to the inevitable, disowned her marriage to Maximilian, and became the wife of Charles VIII [138].

Once again Henry refused to give up, for withdrawal at this stage would have been as ignominious as defeat. On learning of Charles's marriage to Anne, he wrote to the Pope and the German princes urging them to join an anti-French coalition, on the grounds that Maximilian's honour had been slighted. Moreover, through the mediation of his agent in Brittany – a Morlaix lawyer called Pierre le Pennec – Henry indicated his support for a group of dissident Breton nobles who planned a *coup d'état* to install a new government under a new Duke. The plan envisaged the surrender of the Breton ports of Brest and Morlaix to the English in June 1492, so that troops could be landed there. However, Henry apparently thought better of the project, for he suddenly abandoned the plan. He may have feared that Pennec had told too many people about it. If so, his fears were justified, for in August 1492 the plot was betrayed by one of the conspirators [139].

Meanwhile, Charles VIII was busy fomenting his own plot against Henry. In October 1491 Perkin Warbeck, the son of a Tournai Customs officer, had landed at Cork in Ireland with a merchant to whom he was apprenticed. There he was spotted by Yorkist conspirators who thought he might serve their turn. They persuaded him to impersonate Richard, Duke of York – one of the two children of Edward IV murdered in the Tower – and paraded him through the streets as Richard IV. Once again the Lord Deputy, the Earl of Kildare, failed to support Henry. On learning of the appearance of this latest imposter, and of Kildare's inaction, Henry despatched a small body of troops to Ireland which joined with the Butlers – the sworn enemies of the Geraldines – to remove Kildare from office. Warbeck himself escaped, however, and made his way to the French court, where he was welcomed by Charles VIII.

Before Charles could make use of this latest acquisition, Henry struck home. In October 1492 he landed at Calais with an army of over 12,000 men, and proceeded to invest Boulogne. The decision to escalate the war at a time when Charles VIII seemed to hold most of the trump cards might seem uncharacteristically rash, but Henry's principal objective was not to fight but to force France to the negotiating table. This was why he had launched his invasion so late in the year, when the campaigning season was drawing to a close. Henry was presumably aware that Charles VIII had set his heart on invading Italy and would rather settle his dispute with the English king peacefully than waste time and money fighting him. Henry was following the precedent set by Edward IV, who conducted a magnificent foray into France (for which Parliament provided the money) and was rewarded by the Treaty of Picquigny (1475), which guaranteed him a pension for the rest of his life. Henry could also have been hoping that his open challenge to the French king would win him prestige at home and help obscure the fact that he had failed to achieve his main aim of restoring Breton independence.

For his part, Charles was only too willing to allow Henry to save face. After all, by marrying Anne he had not only drawn Brittany into the French sphere of influence, but had ensured that it would eventually be incorporated into his kingdom. Agreement was reached in November 1492, with the conclusion of the Treaty of Etaples. Charles promised not to aid Yorkist pretenders to the English throne, in return for Henry's promise to withdraw his forces from Brittany. Charles also agreed not merely to renew the French pension (which had not been paid since 1482), but also to meet the costs of the English expedition to Brittany in 1489–90 which Duchess Anne had promised to reimburse. All these commitments amounted to £159,000, which France agreed to pay at the rate of £5,000 a year. This was a significant addition to Henry's annual income, yet it was only part of the profit he made on his military ventures. The invasion of France had cost him £48,802, but the Benevolence of 1491 and the parliamentary grants of 1489 and 1491 brought in approximately £181,500. This meant that, quite apart from the French pension, Henry had succeeded in making a substantial net gain. As Professor Alexander has observed, 'Paradoxically, it was his oft-derided invasion of France that caused him to attain a position of complete solvency' [18 *p. 104*]. Even in non-financial terms, Henry's policy had been quite successful. Admittedly, he had failed to preserve the independence of Brittany, but he had gained a Spanish alliance and had helped to secure Burgundy from potentially dangerous French interference.

HABSBURG SUPPORT FOR YORKIST PRETENDERS AND THE PROBLEM OF THE CASTILIAN SUCCESSION

The end of the war with France meant that Henry was now free to deal with Warbeck, who had taken refuge with Margaret, Dowager Duchess of Burgundy. In 1493 the Archduke Maximilian succeeded his father as Holy Roman Emperor, and his son, Philip, took over the government of the Netherlands. During the summer of 1493,

Philip received an embassy from England informing him that Margaret was harbouring an imposter, but he chose to ignore this. Philip was supported by his father, for despite deserting Henry in February 1490, Maximilian was angry with the King for making a separate peace with France. When Henry heard that Burgundy had provided an army of 1,500 mercenaries for Warbeck, he banished all Flemish merchants from England and imposed an embargo on trade with the Netherlands. This action threatened to harm English interests as much as Burgundian, but Henry attempted to minimise the damage by instructing the Merchant Adventurers, who handled cloth exports, to move their staple – that is their main trading outlet – from Antwerp to Calais.

Henry also dealt ruthlessly with potential rebels at home, for his intelligence network had made him aware that some of his leading subjects were secretly in touch with Warbeck. In 1494 his agents penetrated a ring which included the Lord Chamberlain, Sir William Stanley, and a former Lord Steward, Lord FitzWalter. In June 1493 Stanley sent Sir Robert Clifford on a clandestine mission to the court of Margaret of Burgundy – possibly to discover whether Warbeck really was one of Edward IV's sons, and therefore conceivably deserving of Stanley's loyalty. Whatever Stanley's motives, he was arrested in January 1495 and executed the following month. The evidence against him was provided by Clifford, who was pardoned and given £500. FitzWalter was sent prisoner to Calais and only executed after he tried to escape.

Henry's embargo on trade with Burgundy could not prevent Warbeck invading England, but when, in July 1495, he landed at Deal, his tiny expeditionary force was quickly overcome. Warbeck managed to escape to Ireland, where he enlisted the aid of the Earl of Desmond, but his hopes of capturing Waterford were frustrated by Sir Edward Poynings (see above, p. 50), and he thereupon took ship for Scotland.

Warbeck's departure from Burgundy had opened the way to the establishment of friendly relations between Henry and Philip, neither of whom wished to prolong the trade war. In February 1496 they signed the *Magnus Intercursus*, which removed trading barriers between their two states. However, the renewal of goodwill did not extend to Maximilian. The main reason for this was Henry's refusal to join the League of Venice, which had been formed in March 1495 by the Empire, Spain, Milan, Venice and the Papal States to oppose the French invasion of Italy. England had no strategic interests in that area, nor did Henry wish to jeopardise the French pension he had been receiving since Etaples [*Doc. 18*]. Maximilian, on the other hand, believed that England could play a key role in the coalition by invading France, and he was prepared to use Warbeck as a lever to put pressure on Henry. The King tried to reassure him by joining the alliance in 1496 – when it was relaunched as the Holy League – but only on condition that he would not be obliged to declare war on France or to subsidise her enemies. This failed to satisfy Maximilian, who wanted Henry to join in a concerted attack on France, following the sudden death of Charles VIII in 1498. But Henry preferred to retain the friendship of France, particularly since its new ruler was Louis XII, who, as Duke of Orleans, had come to the support of the Bretons.

Henry ultimately paid a high price for his failure to placate Maximilian, who continued to offer refuge to Yorkist pretenders. In 1501 Edmund de la Pole, Earl of Suffolk, fled to Maximilian's court. Suffolk, known as the 'White Rose', was the brother of the Earl of Lincoln, nephew and chosen successor of Richard III, who had been killed at Stoke. He therefore had a strong claim to the throne, and his challenge was all the more serious in view of the death of two of Henry's three sons, Prince Edmund in 1500 and Prince Arthur in 1502. Moreover, 1503 saw the demise of Henry's wife, Elizabeth of York, daughter of Edward IV. Following this catalogue of misfortune, the future of the Tudor dynasty depended upon the survival of the King's second son, Prince Henry, who was unmarried. Henry VII was therefore understandably alarmed by Suffolk's escape, and although the Earl himself was out of reach, all those suspected of involvement in his flight, including his brother, William de la Pole, and the Governor of Guisnes, Sir James Tyrell, were arrested. Many of them, including Tyrell, were subsequently attainted and executed, and in January 1504 Parliament passed Acts forbidding unauthorised assemblies and providing heavy penalties for those who let prisoners escape. The atmosphere of these years is recaptured by an informer's report to the Council of a discussion held among 'many great personages' at Calais. They were considering what would happen after Henry VII's death, and the informant recalled how 'some of them spake of my lord of Buckingham, saying that he was a noble man and would be a royal ruler. Other there were that spake in like wise of your traitor, Edmund de la Pole; but none of them spake of my lord prince' [9 *pp. 5–6*].

Suffolk's presence at the Burgundian court enabled Maximilian and his son, Philip of Burgundy, in effect to blackmail Henry, and between 1505 and 1509 they extracted at least £260,000 from him by way of 'loans' which were never repaid [93]. As far as Henry was concerned, it was worth paying for the protection of his dynasty, but in order to meet the extortionate demands of the Habsburgs, Henry was forced to become an extortioner himself, raising large sums of money from his leading subjects through bonds and recognisances (see above, pp. 29–30). Philip and Maximilian used their ill-gotten gains to finance their dynastic ambitions in Spain. The death of Isabella of Castile in November 1504 threatened to break Spain apart, for her marriage to Ferdinand of Aragon in 1469 had created a union of crowns but not a union of states. Isabella bequeathed Castile to her daughter Joanna, who was married to Philip of Burgundy. Philip claimed to be king consort, and in 1505 he prepared an expedition to Spain to assert his own and his wife's rights. The cost of this expedition, some £138,000, was to be met by Henry VII.

Henry did not dare risk refusing to pay, but he had no desire to turn his friendship with Ferdinand into enmity. The alliance with Spain, which had given him pride and pleasure, had culminated in the marriage of his eldest son and heir, Prince Arthur, to Catherine of Aragon, second daughter of Ferdinand and Isabella. The marriage took place in November 1501, and although Arthur died in the following April, the King rapidly concluded a new agreement whereby Catherine would marry Arthur's younger brother, Prince Henry. This could not be done at once, however, since a papal dispensation was needed to set aside the law of the Church that forbade a man to marry his brother's widow. The marriage had still not taken place by the time Isabella's death brought into question the survival of Spain as a single state. An alliance with Aragon alone would be of limited value, and Prince Henry might be better disposed of elsewhere. In order to gain time and see how things worked out, the King professed to have scruples of conscience about the marriage and instructed the Prince, in 1505, to declare that the treaty was null since it had been made against his will, when he was under age. A further consideration was that the full dowry had not yet been handed over by Spain, and Henry VII was hoping that this apparent drawing-back might encourage Ferdinand to pay the full amount promptly.

Henry's assessment of the situation created by the death of Isabella led him to throw his weight behind Philip of Burgundy's bid for the Castilian throne. Ferdinand was unpopular with the Castilian nobility, and it seemed inevitable that Philip would ultimately win the contest with his elderly father-in-law. There was also the need, on Henry's part, to preserve and foster good commercial relations with Burgundy, for Antwerp had resumed its place as the principal market for English cloth. Finally, Henry could hope that open support for Philip would encourage the Archduke to banish Suffolk, still a major threat to the Tudor dynasty. Luck was on Henry's side, for in January 1506 the ship carrying Philip to Castile was driven by violent storms into Weymouth. The King promptly invited Philip to Windsor, where he persuaded his guest to come to an agreement on all outstanding matters. Under the terms of the secret Treaty of Windsor, signed in February, Henry promised to recognise Philip as King of Castile and to marry Philip's sister, Margaret of Savoy. In return, Philip committed himself to surrender Suffolk. He also empowered his attendant advisers to negotiate the so-called *Malus Intercursus* (see above, p. 68), a commercial treaty that was deeply unfavourable to the Burgundians.

Despite this promising beginning, Henry's attempt to turn the Castilian succession question to his own advantage was largely a failure. His only significant gain was the surrender of Suffolk, who became a prisoner in the Tower and remained there until his execution in 1513. The *Malus Intercursus* was never ratified by Burgundy, and Margaret of Savoy refused to marry Henry, despite pressure to do so from her father, the Emperor Maximilian. Moreover, the unexpected death of Philip in September 1506, while he was in Castile, brought about the collapse of Henry's diplomatic house of cards. Since Philip's son, Charles, was a mere six years old, Ferdinand was able to assume the regency of Castile, thereby ensuring that Spain would remain united.

Finding that he had backed the wrong horse, Henry attempted to retrieve his losses by offering to marry Philip's widow, Joanna, whose lack of mental balance had become acute after the loss of her husband. No doubt Henry was calculating that Ferdinand would welcome this proposal, since it would effectively remove a possible rival from the Spanish scene, but Ferdinand in fact rejected it. Almost as bad, from Henry's point of view, he refused to complete the payment of Catherine of Aragon's dowry. The truth was that Ferdinand no longer needed English friendship. In October 1505, when the struggle with Philip had made him desperate for allies, he had abandoned his traditional anti-French stance and come to terms with Louis XII in the Treaty of Blois. The new relationship was sealed by a marriage between Ferdinand and Louis's niece, Germaine de Foix.

During the closing years of his reign Henry endeavoured to isolate Ferdinand by strengthening his ties with both Burgundy and France. In return for Henry's abandonment of the *Malus Intercursus* and return to the generally acceptable *Magnus Intercursus*, Margaret of Savoy, the regent of the Netherlands, agreed in December 1507 that her nephew Charles, the new Duke of Burgundy, should in due course marry Henry's younger daughter, Mary. Henry also proposed to strengthen his links with France by marrying Prince Henry to another of Louis XII's nieces. In the event, however, all these diplomatic initiatives collapsed, leaving Henry isolated. In December 1508 the Emperor Maximilian, Ferdinand of Spain, Louis XII of France, Charles of Burgundy and the Pope all came together in the League of Cambrai, aimed against Venice. Only Henry VII was excluded.

SCOTLAND

Henry inherited a potentially dangerous situation with respect to his northern neighbour, James III of Scotland. The outstanding problem was Scottish hostility towards the continuing English occupation of Berwick and Dunbar, which had been seized during Edward IV's war with Scotland in 1480–83. In September 1484 Richard III had agreed a three-year truce with the Scots, but Henry VII fully expected them to ignore this and take advantage of the confused situation in England following Bosworth. His fears were justified, for in the summer of 1486 the Scots attacked Dunbar and recaptured the city. Henry made no attempt to save it. He was fully occupied at home, and he may have reasoned that Dunbar, which was close to the Scottish capital, Edinburgh, was too far removed for England to hold on to indefinitely. His abandonment of Dunbar paved the way for peace, particularly since James III also wanted a negotiated settlement and was seeking an English bride after the death of his first wife. A further three-year truce was agreed in July 1486 and both sides appointed commissioners to resolve the outstanding problem of Berwick, still in English hands. By November 1487 sufficient progress had been made for a meeting to be arranged between the two sovereigns in the following July. This never took place, however, for civil war erupted in Scotland and James was defeated and killed at Sauchieburn in June 1488 [144].

This defeat proved to be a major setback for Henry VII as well, and led ultimately to a deterioration in Anglo-Scottish relations. Following Sauchieburn, key supporters of James III took refuge in

England, among them James Ramsay, former Earl of Bothwell. Henry's decision to harbour these men was sensible, for they could always be used to stir up trouble in Scotland if the new government there proved uncooperative. But it prompted the Scots to take counter action by giving shelter to Viscount Lovell and other Yorkists who had escaped the slaughter at Stoke. In addition to providing a safe haven for Yorkist fugitives, Scotland sought to draw tighter its traditional links with France at a time when Henry was seriously contemplating war with that country over Brittany. Moreover, the Scottish government, now dominated by Patrick Hepburn who had usurped the title of Earl of Bothwell, showed no interest in securing an English bride for the new King, James IV, who was still a minor. On the contrary, it was engaged in a search for foreign suitors. Given these circumstances it is hardly surprising that when, at the beginning of 1489, the Master of Huntly led a rebellion against Bothwell, Henry responded to his request for aid by secretly sending James Ramsay with a boatload of munitions to Dumbarton Castle, where the rebels had ensconced themselves [145; 146]. He might well have committed himself more fully had it not been for the other demands made upon his resources. In April 1489 he despatched an expedition to Brittany, and in the same month he had to find troops to put down a rising in the north of England. Moreover, the death of the Earl of Northumberland, killed in a tax riot at Thirsk (see above, p. 19), deprived Henry of the man he needed to rally the northern levies against the Scots.

Henry's limited support of Huntly failed in its objectives, for Dumbarton Castle was captured by the Scots, along with Ramsay. Nevertheless, Henry did not abandon his efforts to undermine the Scottish regime. In late April 1491, while Bothwell was in France, seeking to renew the 'auld alliance', Henry signed an agreement with the anglophile Earl of Angus, who bound himself to attack anyone opposed to a settlement with England. By the beginning of 1492, Angus and his followers had managed to oust Bothwell from power, and thereafter relations between England and Scotland markedly improved. Negotiations were reopened and a nine-year truce was agreed upon. But at this stage, unfortunately for Henry, the situation was transformed by the coming-of-age of James IV [145].

The youthful Scottish king was eager to win military glory by renewing the struggle with England, and when, in 1495, the pretender Perkin Warbeck arrived at his court, James gave him not only a royal welcome but also the hand in marriage of his cousin, Lady Catherine Gordon. James promised to assist Warbeck in mounting an invasion of England, on the understanding that once the pretender had made good his claim to the English throne he would not only reimburse James for the cost of the expedition but also hand over Berwick. News of this last concession alienated the English nobles in the northern counties, and the invasion, which was launched in September 1496, proved a fiasco. Most of the Scottish nobles refused to take part, with the result that a mere 1,400 men crossed the border, and although Warbeck called on his 'subjects' to rise against the 'usurper' Henry, there was no response. As soon as the Scottish troops heard that an English force was moving against them, they fled back across the border. Warbeck, who lingered on at the Scottish court until the summer of 1497, remained a potential threat but no longer an immediate danger.

Although Warbeck's invasion had come to nothing, Henry could not ignore the challenge thrown down by James IV. In October 1496 he summoned a Great Council which granted money for the prosecution of a war against the Scots. This was confirmed by Parliament in January 1497, when the members not only voted two Fifteenths and Tenths but added a subsidy 'for their necessary defence against the cruel malice of the Scots'. Henry went ahead with preparations for his campaign [143], but in June 1497, while his armies were mustering in the north, the inhabitants of the west country rose in revolt. They were driven by anger against the levy of taxes for a war to take place at the other end of the kingdom, which meant nothing to them. Although the rebels were poorly led, they surged through the western counties and by the middle of June were encamped on Blackheath, to the south of London. There they encountered Henry's forces, and although they fought bravely, they were heavily defeated. The rebel ringleaders were captured and executed. The rank and file were left to straggle back the way they had come.

James IV took advantage of the Western Rebellion to invade England once again, but his forces were chased back over the border by troops under the Earl of Surrey. This latest reverse was enough to persuade James to sue for peace, and in September 1497 hostilities were ended by the Truce of Ayton. Warbeck left Scotland before it was signed. In July 1497 he landed in Ireland for the third time in six years, hoping to find that country as welcoming as ever to Yorkist pretenders. But the Irish had learnt their lesson. Kildare, who had been restored to his post of Lord Deputy in 1495, now remained loyal to Henry Tudor, while the citizens of Waterford sent out their ships to try to seize the pretender. But Warbeck was already on his way to Cornwall, where he hoped that the disaffection to Henry, demonstrated in the rebellion, would assure him a more favourable reception. He was not disappointed. Resentment was still smouldering in the area, and several thousand men came in to join him. But the King had been warned of Warbeck's arrival, and Daubeney was already on his way west, with a royal army. Warbeck's progress was blocked at Exeter, where the Earl of Devon rallied the citizens behind him and closed the gates against the pretender. When Warbeck heard that Daubeney's forces were closing in on him he abandoned the siege and fled to sanctuary at Beaulieu Abbey near Southampton. There he surrendered, and in early October he appeared before Henry at Taunton, where he made a full confession of his imposture.

Warbeck could hardly have expected merciful treatment at Henry's hands, for he had caused the King more trouble than any other pretender. Yet Henry kept him under mild captivity, and only transferred him to the Tower in 1498, after he had attempted to escape. Warbeck, the false duke, and Warwick, the real earl, were now prisoners together, but they were not permitted to live much longer. Their fate was probably linked to the proposed marriage between Prince Arthur and Catherine of Aragon, since Ferdinand and Isabella were reluctant to send their daughter to England while pretenders still threatened the Tudor dynasty [142]. In 1499, therefore, the two prisoners were put on trial. Warbeck, convicted of plotting to seize the Tower and escape from custody, was hanged at Tyburn. Warwick was found guilty of treason, but his royal blood saved him from a felon's death. Instead, he was beheaded on Tower Hill.

The removal of Warbeck from the scene paved the way for the so-called 'Treaty of Perpetual Peace' with Scotland, which was signed in February 1502. This not only extended the Truce of Ayton but also provided for a marriage between James IV and Henry's eldest daughter, Margaret. On the face of it, the 1502 treaty proved a resounding success, for the marriage took place in August 1503 and the peaceful relations which it symbolised lasted for the rest of Henry's reign. The treaty had its deficiencies, however, the most important being that it left the Franco-Scottish alliance intact. Between 1502 and 1513 James IV lavished funds on building four large warships with the aid of French technicians. These were constructed not simply for defensive reasons but also to demonstrate to France how useful an ally Scotland would be if and when war broke out again between France and England [145].

The Treaty of Perpetual Peace also failed to reduce tension in the border region between England and Scotland. Admittedly it provided for 'days of truce', on which the Wardens of the Marches on both sides would come together to enforce the law, but it was on one of these days that the Scottish Warden of the Middle March, Sir Robert Ker, was killed by an Englishman named John Heron. Despite James IV's protests, Heron was allowed to go free in England. The incident rankled with James, for it headed his list of grievances when Scotland launched another invasion of England in 1513. However, the most serious threat to the maintenance of peace occurred in 1508, when the Earl of Arran, a kinsman of James IV who had been charged with renewing Scotland's alliance with France, was detained in England on his return journey. If Henry was hoping thereby to undermine the Franco-Scottish accord, his action threatened to have quite the opposite effect. Henry had to despatch his almoner, Thomas Wolsey, to Edinburgh to resolve matters peacefully. Wolsey advised Arran's immediate release, and Henry complied, but the episode showed how fragile was the relationship between England and her northern neighbour [145]. In the words of Professor MacDougall, 'it can hardly be said that the Treaty of Perpetual Peace, less than seven years after its creation, was proving a resounding success' [145 *p. 256*]. It was perhaps fortunate for Henry that he died in 1509. Had he lived a few years longer he would have seen the complete unravelling of his settlement with Scotland.

PART THREE: ASSESSMENT

11 CONCLUSION

When John Richard Green published his *Short History of the English People* in 1874, he entitled the chapter which dealt with events from 1471 to 1509 'The New Monarchy'. He made his reasons for doing so perfectly clear. English constitutional development, as he saw it, had been progressing very nicely under the Lancastrians, with the liberties of the subject protected and strengthened by an active Parliament, a time-honoured system of law with which no mere ruler could interfere, and the beginnings of commercial expansion. All this was brought to an end by the Wars of the Roses, for these did 'far more than ruin one royal house or set up another on the throne. If they did not utterly destroy English freedom, they arrested its progress for more than a hundred years'. The people of England had been reaping the benefits of the struggle against medieval autocracy, and had won their freedom from arbitrary taxation, arbitrary imprisonment, and arbitrary legislation. But after the wars had done their destructive work, the power of the crown expanded to such an extent that it stifled individual liberty. 'The character of the monarchy from the time of Edward the Fourth to the time of Elizabeth remains something strange and isolated in our history. It is hard to connect the kingship of the old English, of the Norman, the Angevin, or the Plantagenet Kings, with the kingship of the House of York or the House of Tudor'.

Green's *Short History* was so influential, and its 'liberal' assumptions so in tune with the presuppositions of his age, that his interpretation gained general acceptance. All that later historians did was to modify some of the details, and in the textbooks, at any rate, 1485 rather than 1471 was taken as the date at which the 'New Monarchy' began. The advantage of making a break at 1485 was that it linked the arrival of a new dynasty on the English throne with the more widespread changes that were transforming European society from 'medieval' to 'modern'. Henry VII coincided with the Renaissance, and his son brought the Reformation to England. By these tokens they were obviously 'new monarchs', far removed in their methods and their philosophy from their predecessors on the English throne.

The characteristics of this Tudor 'New Monarchy', as they were defined by later historians, were solvency, efficiency, autocratic centralisation, the development of the household at the expense of the older, more 'public' institutions, and the use of 'middle-class' men in place of feudal aristocrats. So far as Henry VII is concerned, his solvency is beyond question. Moreover, his government was efficient by contemporary standards; it focused power upon the centre; and it was autocratic to the extent that it elevated royal authority and used a wide range of prerogative institutions and practices. It is also the case that it worked through household institutions like the Chamber, rather than 'public' ones such as the Exchequer, and that it relied on the gentry as much as – if not more than – the aristocracy to carry the King's commands into effect. In all these ways, then, Henry VII seems to conform to the pattern of a 'new monarch' and the battle of Bosworth can be held to signal the beginning of a new era in English history.

There is, however, another side to the picture. Solvency seems to have been characteristic only of Henry VII, not of the Tudors in general. As for efficiency, a great deal depends upon the meaning attached to this term. Henry VII's government was certainly more effective than Henry VI's, but this did not mean that it was radically different from its medieval predecessors: the governments of Henry II and Edward I, for example, were formidably efficient. Moreover, procrastination, deviousness and incapacity were not totally eliminated by the first Tudor; even in the financial sphere, where improvement was most marked, the absence of systematisation led to overlapping and duplication.

There are certainly centralising tendencies to be observed in Henry VII's administration, but what strikes a modern observer is the way in which power was decentralised rather than concentrated. The facts of geography and poor communications were largely responsible for this, since they compelled the King to devolve responsibility to the men on the spot. The Council could advise and encourage, warn and threaten, but in the last analysis Henry was dependent upon the co-operation of the political nation, the propertied section of English society.

The same is true where Henry's autocratic tendencies are concerned. He may have wished to rule in the 'French manner', and he gave his Court a degree of formality which emphasised the greatness of his majesty. But Henry was never an absolute monarch. He was limited by custom and by law, and even had he wished to sweep away these barriers he could not have done so. He had no police force and no standing army. In time of danger even more than in time of peace he was dependent upon the support of the property-owners.

Henry's development of household administration and his reliance on 'middle-class' men are often cited as the most novel features of his rule, but neither of these was 'new'. Medieval administration had never been confined to great public offices such as Chancery and the Exchequer: during the reign of Edward III, for instance, the Wardrobe had expanded into a *de facto* national treasury, much as the Chamber did under Henry VII. If there was nothing particularly new about Henry's use of household departments to by-pass established institutions, the same is true of his increasing use of gentry to run his government. Such men were not 'middle-class': the term was unknown, as was the concept. The gentry were an integral part of the upper section of English society and were 'new' only in the sense that their families had not previously been prominent in national, as distinct from local, government. They were advancing by a route which many had taken before them. Henry I, to mention only one of many examples, was accused of raising men from the dust to serve him, and it may be taken for a general rule that the 'new men' whom one king chose for his service founded aristocratic families which asserted a natural and exclusive right to counsel his successors.

Henry VII did not begin his reign with a clean slate. The machinery of medieval government had survived the period of disorder, and Henry was probably only too thankful to make use of it. The job of ruling late-medieval England was far from easy, and institutions which had stood the test of time offered the best means of doing so, for their very longevity made them acceptable. New methods might have been better in theory, but were likely to arouse intense resentment, for as a Venetian observer acutely noted, 'If the King of England should propose to change any old-established rule, it would seem to every Englishman as if his life were taken away from him' [65 *p. 155*]. Henry did not have the doubtful advantage of knowing that the Middle Ages were over and that it was his historically appointed task to lead his country into a new epoch. For him the problems of government were much as they had always been. So were the solutions. All that was needed was to make the existing system work properly.

From the beginning of his reign until the end Henry deliberately exploited the rights of the crown in order to make it once again rich and powerful. It may be that in his later years, when he was securely established on the throne, he acted in a more high-handed fashion and disregarded or overrode the rights and liberties of his subjects. But it can be argued just as convincingly that the real change took place not in Henry's policy but in the attitude of the property-owners. They had been prepared to pay a high price for the restoration of good order after the breakdown of the late fifteenth century, but as they came to take more settled conditions for granted they increasingly resented the remorseless pressure of the royal administration and complained about its injustices [*Doc. 11*]. There is little point in trying to distribute praise or blame. Henry VII, as King, was determined to restore the financial health of the crown, and if, in working towards this end, he and his servants sometimes behaved in an arbitrary manner, it has to be borne in mind that failure to act effectively would have meant a return to anarchy. As for the property-owners, by their determination to hold on to what they regarded as rightfully theirs, they drove government to the very excesses of which they bitterly complained. Yet at the same time, and by the same determination, they preserved legal and political liberties which in other countries were being eroded by the power of the state.

Henry VII cannot be neatly fitted into categories of 'new' or 'old', 'modern' or 'medieval'. He has gone down to history as the first Tudor, but he seems to have thought of himself as a Lancastrian. He had a particular respect for Henry VI – whom he always referred to as his uncle – and showed this by renewing work upon the chapel at King's College, Cambridge, which the martyred king had begun. In his will, Henry VII ordered that the work should be carried through to completion 'for the singular trust that we have to the prayers of our said uncle, for the great holiness of life and virtue that he was of in earth' [16 *pp. 27–8*]. He had originally intended to provide a magnificent tomb for Henry VI at Windsor, but was persuaded that Westminster Abbey would be a more appropriate resting place. Henry VI was therefore to be interred in the Lady Chapel, which Henry VII intended to build and where he planned to be buried [*Doc. 19*]. A further reason for Henry VII's choice of the Lady Chapel for his own 'perpetual sepulture' was that it already contained 'the body of our graunt Dame of right noble memory Queen Kateryne, wife to King Henry the Vth and daughter to King Charles of France' [16 *p. 3*]. There is no suggestion here that Henry wished to be regarded as the founder of a new ruling house.

In fact, the establishment of the Tudor dynasty owed as much to luck as to calculation. If Prince Henry had followed his brother Arthur to the grave, the peaceful accession of Henry's eldest daughter Margaret could not have been taken for granted. Civil war might well have broken out again, and Henry VII would be remembered, if at all, simply as one more in the succession of late medieval rulers who tried in vain to restore the strength of the monarchy, and with it good order and government. No ruler, however successful, could hope to eradicate in the space of a single reign the evils that afflicted contemporary England. Large bands of retainers were not unknown even in Elizabeth's day; 'bastard feudalism' was positively encouraged by Henry VIII when, for example, he made the Russells the greatest family in the west country; and as for rioting and turbulence, these remained features of English life for several centuries after Henry VII's death.

Even in the more general context of the shift from 'medieval' to 'modern' Henry VII's reign marks no decisive break, for communities change gradually, and different aspects change at different rates. The supremacy of the Catholic Church, which had been characteristic of the Middle Ages, survived Henry VII by less than one generation, but villeinage and wardship lingered on into the seventeenth century. As for such medieval institutions as the courts of King's Bench and Common Pleas, these maintained their independent existence well into the nineteenth century, while grand juries survived in England until the twentieth. No one would deny today that medieval England has long since vanished, but many of its features, at least in their outward form, are with us still. The monarchy survives, although its functions have been radically curtailed. So do Parliament and the common law.

The mixture of old and new in Henry's monarchy is symbolised by his tomb. In 1506, when he was considering the style in which he would be consigned to history, Henry chose as his sculptor Guido Mazzoni of Modena, who produced a design unlike anything seen in England before. In fact the tomb was only built after Henry's death, and the work was carried out not by Mazzoni but by another Italian, Pietro Torrigiano of Florence. The sarcophagus itself, with the recumbent figures of Henry and his wife, Elizabeth of York, is Renaissance in inspiration and heralds the arrival in England of the new style that was transforming European art. Around the sarcophagus, however, is an exquisite bronze screen, the work of an English craftsman, Humphrey Walker, who designed it in the Perpendicular style which was England's unique contribution to

Gothic architecture. To think of Henry VII as a Renaissance monarch confined within a late medieval setting is to come close to understanding the significance of his reign.

PART FOUR: DOCUMENTS

A DESCRIPTION OF HENRY VII

His body was slender but well built and strong; his height above the average. His appearance was remarkably attractive and his face was cheerful, especially when speaking; his eyes were small and blue, his teeth few, poor and blackish; his hair was thin and white; his complexion sallow. His spirit was distinguished, wise and prudent; his mind was brave and resolute, and never, even at moments of the greatest danger, deserted him. He had a most pertinacious memory. Withal he was not devoid of scholarship. In government he was shrewd and prudent, so that no one dared to get the better of him through deceit or guile. He was gracious and kind and was as attentive to his visitors as he was easy of access. His hospitality was splendidly generous; he was fond of having foreigners at his court and he freely conferred favours on them. But those of his subjects who were indebted to him and who did not pay him due honour or who were generous only with promises, he treated with harsh severity. He well knew how to maintain his royal majesty and all which appertains to kingship at every time and in every place. He was most fortunate in war, although he was constitutionally more inclined to peace than to war. He cherished justice above all things; as a result he vigorously punished violence, manslaughter and every other kind of wickedness whatsoever. Consequently he was greatly regretted on that account by all his subjects, who had been able to conduct their lives peaceably, far removed from the assaults and evil doing of scoundrels. He was the most ardent supporter of our faith, and daily participated with great piety in religious services. To those whom he considered to be worthy priests, he often secretly gave alms so that they should pray for his salvation. He was particularly fond of those Franciscan friars whom they call Observants, for whom he founded many convents, so that with his help their rule should continually flourish in his kingdom. But all these virtues were obscured latterly only by avarice, from which ... he suffered. This avarice is surely a bad enough vice in a private individual, whom it forever torments; in a monarch indeed it may be considered the worst vice, since it is harmful to everyone, and distorts those qualities of trustfulness, justice and integrity by which the state must be governed.

Polydore Vergil, [15], pp. 145–7.

DOCUMENT 2   **WARDSHIP**

November 20, 1495: Grant to William Martyn, esquire, and William Twynyho, esquire, of the keeping of the lands late of John Trenchard, tenant in chief, and after the death of Margaret, widow of the said John, of the lands which she holds in dower; with the wardship and marriage of Thomas Trenchard, his son and heir.

October 3, 1487: Item, received of Richard Harp, receiver-general of the Duchy of Lancaster, for the ward and marriage of Humfrey Hill, £20.

February 26, 1503: Item, to Sir Richard Guilford in full payment of £200 for finding of the ward of Francis Cheyne, £30.

May 10, 1503: Item, received of Sir Reginald Bray for the ward and marriage of the two daughters of ... Lovell of Sussex, £140.

Richardson, [51], pp. 166–7.

DOCUMENT 3   **A FORCED LOAN, 1486**

The king sent my lord Treasurer with master Bray and other honourable personages unto the mayor, requiring him and his citizens of a loan of vi thousand marks [i.e. £4,000], wherefore the mayor assembled his brethren and the Common Council upon the Tuesday following. By whose authority was then granted to the king a loan of £2,000, the which for him was shortly levied after, and this was assessed by the fellowships and not by the wards, for the more ease of the poor people. Of the which loan the fellowships of mercers, grocers and drapers lent £ixCxxxvii. vis. The which loan was justly repaid in the year following.

Fabian, [10], p. 240.

DOCUMENT 4   **PARLIAMENTARY SUPPLY, 1491**

To the worship of God: we your Commons, by your high commandment come to this your present Parliament for the shires, cities and burghs of this your noble realm, calling to our remembrance the great continued zeal, love and tenderness which your royal person hath to defend this your realm and all your subjects of the same ... and that ye verily intending, as we understand ... in your most noble person to invade upon your and our ancient enemies with an army royal ... to subdue by the might of God your and our said ancient enemies to the weal of you and prosperity of this your realm; so that your said highness might have therein of us your said Commons loving assistance; for the which we, your said Commons, by the assent of the Lords spiritual and temporal in this your present Parliament assembled, grant by this present indenture to you our sovereign liege lord, for the necessary defence of this your said realm, and us your said true subjects of the same, ii whole xv^{mes} and x^{mes} to be had, paid, taken and levied of the moveable goods, chattels and other things usually to such xv^{mes} and x^{mes} contributory and chargeable within the shires, cities, burghs and towns and other places of this your said realm, in manner and form aforetime used.

7 Henry VII c. 11. *The Statutes of the Realm*, Vol. II (1817), p. 555.

DOCUMENT 5   BENEVOLENCES

The king – lest the poorer sort should be burdened with the charge of paying the troops for the war – levied money from the rich only, each contributing to the pay of the troops according to his means. Since it was the responsibility of each individual to contribute a great or a small sum, this type of tax was called a 'benevolence'. Henry in this copied King Edward IV, who first ... raised money from the people under the name of loving kindness. In this process it could be perceived precisely how much each person cherished the king – something which it had not before been possible to observe – for the man who paid most was presumed to be most dutiful; many none the less secretly grudged their contribution, so that this method of taxation might more appropriately be termed a 'malevolence' rather than a 'benevolence'. However, since no one would have it said he was less dutiful, all competed to pay the required money.

Polydore Vergil, [15], p. 49.

DOCUMENT 6   DECREES OF THE COUNCIL IN STAR
            CHAMBER

Sir Thomas Worthy and others are ordered to place Robert Inkarsall and Sibilla his wife in possession, and when they have been so placed to defend them by the authority of the lord King and in the name of His Majesty, and to cause them to be defended to the utmost of their power against John Parker and William Parker and any others whomsoever. Because the said complainants were riotously and violently disseised by the defendants themselves. And they are ordered to answer when called on concerning punishment for rioting, and concerning damages, costs and the interest of the parties.

It is decreed that a letter be written by the lord king to the Earl of Surrey, that he himself place John Steward in possession or cause him to be placed in possession. And that when he has been placed in possession he cause him to be defended in that possession in the name of the lord king aforesaid in the case between John Steward and Lady Agnes Coneas, defendant.

Bayne, [3], pp. 25–7 (translated from the Latin original by The Selden Society).

DOCUMENT 7   THE 'STAR CHAMBER' ACT, 1487

The King our sovereign lord remembereth how by unlawful maintenances, giving of liveries, signs and tokens, and retainders by indenture, promises, oaths, writing or otherwise; embraceries* of his subjects, untrue demeanings of sheriffs in making of panels and other untrue returns; by taking of money by juries, by great riots and unlawful assemblies; the policy and good rule of this realm is almost subdued. And for the non punishment of this inconvenience, and by occasion of the premises, nothing or little may be found by enquiry, whereby the laws of the land in execution may take little effect, to the increase of murders, robberies, perjuries and unsureties of all men living, and losses of their lands and goods, to the great displeasure of almighty God. Be it therefore ordained, for reformation of the premises, by the authority of this Parliament, that the Chancellor and Treasurer of England for the time being, and Keeper of the King's Privy Seal, or two of them, calling to him a bishop and a temporal lord of the King's most honourable Council, and the two Chief Justices of the King's Bench and Common Pleas for the time being, or two other justices in their absence, upon bill of information put to the said Chancellor, for the King or any other, against any person for any misbehaving afore rehearsed, have authority to call before them by writ or privy seal the said misdoers, and them and other by their discretions, to whom the truth may be known, to examine; and such as they find therein defective, to punish them after their demerits, after the form and effect of statutes thereof made, in like manner and form as they should and ought to be punished if they were convict after the due order of the law.

*embracery or embracing were terms used to describe the corruption of juries.

3 Henry VII c. 1. *The Statutes of the Realm*, Vol. II (1817), pp. 509–10.

DOCUMENT 8   A CASE BEFORE THE 1487 TRIBUNAL

To the most reverend fader in god the Archebisshop of Caunterbury Chaunceller of England.

Shewith unto your good Lordship James hobart Attorne of the king our

Sovereigne Lord that where oon Robart Carvyle of Tilney in the Shire of
Norfolk the xxix day of June the secund yere of the reigne of our
Sovereigne Lord the King that now is was in his owne propre soyle in Tilne
aforeseid laboryng in makyng hay ther came oon Thomas hunston with
[one] of his servauntes whos name is onknowen in riotouse wise with force
and armes that is to sey with longe knyves a staff and a spere and thane
and ther riotously came out of the high waye into the ground of the seid
Robart and thane and there in to the seid Robart made ther Assaut and
hym bete wounded mayhend and lefte almost dede ageyn the kingis Lawys
and peas. And forasmoch as the seid Robert for salvacon of his Lyff
defended hym self with a sithe which he thanne hadde in his handys to
mowe therwith gresse and in the same defence fortuned with the same sithe
to hurt the seid Thomas the same Thomas hath sued appele of mayhene
ageyn the same Robart in whych appelle the seid Robart pleded to an issue
of the Countre and theruppon xii parcyall men by speciall labour were
impanelled and by craft and sotill menye and also by [gr]ete labour and
inbraciary and by mene of geving of goed unto them were sworn to trye the
seid mater. And by such onlawfull occasions passed ageyn the seid Robart
and taxed damages one C marc ageyn toruth reson and good consciens. for
the verry toruth is that the hurt that the said Thomas hadde was of his
owne assaute and in the defence of the seid Robart to the [utter] undoyng of
the seid Robart and to the right perilous example by which occasion the
seid Robart is so inpoverished that he is not of power to sue his lawfull
remedye after the course of the commen lawe. The tenure of the record of
the seid appelle and the names of the seid xii men to this bill is annexed.
That it may plese your good and gracious lordship in eschewyng of such
opynn and abhominable perjurie in tyme to cum to direct severall writtes of
subpena as well to the seid Thomas as to the seid xii menn comaundyng
them by the same to appere afore your lordship my lord Tresourer and my
lord prive seale or ii of you and other at a certeyn day after theffect and
form of a statute made in the last parliament of our seid sovereigne lord the
tenure of whych statute here after ensueth the seid Thomas and the xii men
and other before you to be examined of ther behavior and demenyng in
passing in the same Jure and therupon to procede and doo in that behalfe as
well for punyssion of the seid Thomas for the seid riot & other
mysbehavinges as all the seid persons which so passed as shall accorde with
reson and your good discresions & with the force and effect of the seid
statute & other statutes afore tyme made. And our blessed Savyor preserve
your good and gracious lordship.

Bayne, [3], pp. 62–3.

DOCUMENT 9   OFFENCES COMMITTED WITHIN THE
KING'S HOUSEHOLD, 1487

AN ACT THAT THE STEWARD, TREASURER AND CONTROLLER OF
THE KING'S HOUSE SHALL ENQUIRE OF OFFENCES DONE WITHIN
THE SAME

For so much as by quarrels made to such as hath been in great authority, office
and of council with Kings of this realm, hath ensued the destruction of
Kings and the near undoing of this realm ... and for the most part it hath
grown and been occasioned by envy and malice of the King's own
household servants ... and for so much as by the law of this land, if actual
deeds be not had, there is no remedy for such false compassings,
imaginations and confederacies, had against any lord of any of the King's
Council or any of the King's great officers in his household, as Steward,
Treasurer, Controller, and so great inconveniences might ensue if such
ungodly demeanor should not be straitly punished, or the actual deed were
done, therefore be it ordered ... that from henceforward the Steward,
Treasurer and Controller of the King's House ... have full authority and
power to enquire by twelve sad [i.e. wise] and discreet persons of the check
roll of the King's honourable household, if any servant admitted to be his
servant in his house ... under the state of a lord, make any confederacies,
compassings, conspiracies, imaginations with any person or persons to
destroy or murder the King or any lord of this realm or any Steward,
Treasurer, Controller of the King's house ... he so found by the enquiry be
put thereupon to answer. And the Steward, Treasurer and Controller, or
two of them, have power to determine the same matter according to the
law. And if he put him in trial, that then it be tried by other twelve sad men
of the same household. ... And if such misdoers be found guilty ... that the
said offence be judged felony and they to have judgment and execution as
felons attainted owe to have by the common law.

3 Henry VII c. 14. *The Statutes of the Realm*, Vol. II (1817), p. 521.

DOCUMENT 10   DUDLEY'S ACCOUNT BOOK, SEPTEMBER
1504–MAY 1508

Item, £20 in money for Robert Marshall to be receiver in Norfolk, Suffolk
and Cambridgeshire, as Robert Strange was.

Item, delivered for the grant of the goods and chattels of one John
Chauncy, forfeited by reason of an outlawry, £20 – *viz.* ten pounds in ready
money and £10 by obligation.

Item, delivered the indenture between the king's grace and Lewes de la
ffava concerning the lease of his royal ship called the Regent, and the
customs outward and homeward of the said ship, for the which the said

Lewes must pay to our said sovereign lord as in the same indenture appeareth for several causes the sum of five thousand and one hundred pounds.

Item, delivered for the Bishop of Lincoln for discharge of a fine of eight hundred marks for his mill and fishweirs upon the river Trent, three hundred pounds – *viz.* £100 in ready money, and £200 by obligation.

Richardson, [51], p. 156.

DOCUMENT 11   **THE REACTION AGAINST EMPSON AND DUDLEY AFTER THE DEATH OF HENRY VII**

AN ACT FOR ADMITTANCE OF A TRAVERS AGAINST AN UNTRUE INQUISITION

Sheweth unto your discreet wisdoms that where divers and many untrue inquisitions by the procurement of Richard Empson, knight, and Edmond Dudley, have be had and take within this realm as well before commissioners assigned by letters patents of the late king, King Henry vii[th], as before his exchetours, as well by virtue of writs of the said late king as by virtue of their office, by the which inquisitions sometime parcel of the said lands contained in the said inquisitions and sometime the hole lands there founden holden of the said late king *in capite*, where in truth the said lands contained in the said inquisitions nor no parcel of them was hold of the said late king *in capite* ne of any of his progenitors; to the which inquisitions the parties then grieved by the same could not nor might not take their travers to the same* according to the law of this land, but were inforced and constrained to sue their livery of the same out of the hands of the said late king, whereby they were and be concluded to say but that the said lands be holden of the king in chief, to their great loss and hindrance, where in truth they were not holden of the said late king ne of any of his progenitors.

Wherefore be it enacted, ordained and established by the king our sovereign lord and the lords spiritual and temporal and the commons in this present parliament assembled, and by the authority of the same, that every person and persons having possession of the said lands contained in the same inquisitions or any part thereof may be admitted to have their travers to the said untrue inquisitions, notwithstanding any livery sued of the same in the time of the said late king, King Harry the vii[th].

* 'to take their travers' is to make a formal denial of the charge.

1 Henry VIII c. 12. *The Statutes of the Realm*, Vol. III (1817), p. 7.

DOCUMENT 12   AN INDENTURE OF RETAINDER

This indenture made the xxv day of April the xxi year of the reign of King Edward the IV [i.e. 1481] between William Hastings, knight, Lord Hastings, on the one part, and Ralph Longford, esquire, on the other part, witnesseth that the said Ralph agreeth, granteth, and by these present indentures bindeth him to the said lord to be his retained servant during his life, and to him to do faithful and true service, and the part of the same lord take against all men in peace and war with as many persons defensibly arrayed as the same Ralph can or may make at all times that the said lord will command him, at the said lord's costs and charges, saving the allegiance which the same Ralph oweth to the king our sovereign lord and to the prince. And the said lord granteth to the said Ralph to be his good and favourable lord and him aid and support in his right according to the law. In witness hereof the foresaid parties to these present indentures have interchangeably set their seals and signs manual the day and year aforesaid.

Dunham, [73], p. 132.

DOCUMENT 13   FORM OF A LICENCE TO RETAIN

Henry, by the grace of God, King of England and of France and lord of Ireland – greeting ... WE ... by the advice of our Council, intending to provide a good, substantial and competent number of captains and able men of our subjects to be in a readiness to serve us at our pleasure when the case shall require, and trusting in your faith and truth, will and desire you, and ... by these presents give unto you full power and authority from henceforth during our pleasure to take, appoint and retain by indenture or covenant in form or manner as hereafter ensueth, and none otherwise, such persons our subjects as by your discretion shall be thought and seemeth to you to be able men to do us service in the war in your company under you and at your leading at all times and places and as often as it shall please us to command or assign you, to the number of – persons, whose names be contained in a certificate by you made in a bill of parchment indented betwixt us and you and interchangeably signed by us and subscribed with your hand and to our secretary delivered ... PROVIDED always that you retain not above the said number which you shall indent for in form and manner hereafter ensuing. PROVIDED also the same able persons shall not be chosen, taken nor retained but only of your own tenants or of the inhabitants within any office that you have of our grant. ... And these our present letters shall be unto you, and all and every the persons by you to be retained in form above specified and indented for with us, and such other as you shall retain in the place of any of them died, avoided or discharged as above is specified, sufficient discharge in this behalf at all times hereafter, any act, statute, prohibition or other ordinance in the time of us or any of our noble progenitors or predecessors, by authority of parliament or otherwise, heretofore made, enacted, passed or ordained to the contrary notwithstanding. PROVIDED always that you, under colour hereof or by virtue of these our letters of placard, retain no more in number by word, promise or otherwise than is contained in your said certificate indented and indented for with us as above, under the pains specified in our statutes made and ordained in that behalf.

Dunham, [73], pp. 148–50.

DOCUMENT 14   **BONDS AND RECOGNISANCES**

16 June 1505. [Recognisance] for £2,000 by Henry, Lord Clifford. Condition: Henry to keep the peace for himself and his servants, tenants and 'part takers', especially towards Roger Tempest of Broughton, and endeavour to bring before the King and his Council within 40 days such of his servants as were present at the late pulling down of Roger's place and house at Broughton.

24 December 1507. Indenture between the King and the same George, Lord Burgevenny: whereas George is indebted to the King in £100,000 or thereabouts for unlawful receivers done, retained and made by him in Kent contrary to certain laws and statutes, as was found by inquisitions certified into the King's Bench and adjudged after free confession by him in the said court in Michaelmas term last; and whereas for execution and levy of this debt being clearly due both in law and conscience the King may attach his body and keep him in prison and take all the issues of his lands till the whole sum be paid; the King is graciously contented, at his suit for avoiding the extremity of the law, to accept as parcel of the debt the sum of £5,000 payable over ten years at Candlemas and the Purification; for which payments, as well as the residue of the debt, George binds himself and his heirs.
Given 24 December, 23 Henry VII. Cancelled by warrant, 1 Henry VIII.

Calendar of the Close Rolls, [4], Vol. II, Nos 499 and 825 (iv).

DOCUMENT 15   **AN ACT OF ATTAINDER 1491**

Forasmuch as Sir Robert Chamberleyn, late of Barking in the shire of Essex, knight, and Richard White, late of Thorpe beside Billingforde in the shire of Norfolk, gentleman, the xxiiii day of August, and the said Sir Robert the xvii day of January the vi[th] year of the reign of our sovereign lord the king that now is, at Barking aforesaid traitorously imagined and compassed the death and destruction of our said sovereign lord, and also the subversion of all this realm, then and there traitorously levied war against our said sovereign lord and adhered them traitorously to Charles the French king, ancient enemy to our said sovereign lord and this realm, against their duty and liegance; Be it therefore ordained and enacted by authority of this present Parliament that the said Robert and Richard stand and be attainted of high treason, and forfeit all manors, lands, tenements, rents, reversions and all other hereditaments that they or either of them or any other to their use or to the use of either of them had at any of the said days, of estate of fee simple or fee tail in England or Wales.

3 Henry VII c. 23. *The Statutes of the Realm*, Vol. II (1817), p. 566.

DOCUMENT 16   **AUTO DA FÉ**

Upon the xxviii day of April was an old cankered heretic, weak-minded for age, named Joan Boughton, widow, and mother unto the wife of Sir John Young – which daughter, as some reported, had a great smell of an heretic after the mother – burnt in Smithfield. This woman was iiii score years of age or more, and held viii opinions of heresy which I pass over, for the hearing of them is neither pleasant nor fruitful. She was a disciple of Wyclif, whom she accounted for a saint, and held so fast and firmly viii of his xii opinions that all the doctors [of divinity] of London could not turn her from one of them. When it was told to her that she should be burnt for her obstinacy and false belief, she set nought at their words but defied them, for she said she was so beloved with God and His holy angels that all the fire in London should not hurt her. But on the morrow a bundle of faggots and a few reeds consumed her in a little while; and while she might cry she spake often of God and Our Lady, but no man could cause her to name Jesus, and so she died. But it appeared that she left some of her disciples behind her, for the night following, the more part of the ashes of that fire that she was burnt in were had away and kept for a precious relic in an earthen pot.

Fabian, [10], p. 252.

DOCUMENT 17   **NAVIGATION ACT, 1485**

AN ACT AGAINST BRINGING IN OF GASCON WINE EXCEPT IN ENGLISH, IRISH OR WELSHMEN'S SHIPS

To the right wise and discreet Commons in this present Parliament assembled. Please it your great wisdoms to call to your remembrance of the great minishing and decay that hath been now of late time of the navy within this realm of England, and idleness of the mariners within the same, by the which this noble realm within short process of time, without reformation be had therein, shall not be of ability and power to defend itself. Wherefore please it your great wisdoms to pray the king our sovereign lord that, by the advice of his lords spiritual and temporal, and of you his Commons, in this present Parliament assembled, and by authority of the same, it be enacted, ordained and established that no manner person of what degree or condition that he be of, buy nor sell within this said realm, Ireland, Wales, Calais or the marches thereof, or Berwick, from the feast of Michaelmas next now coming, any manner wines of the growing of the duchy of Guienne or of Gascony, but such as shall be adventured and brought in an English, Irish or Welshman's ship or ships, and the mariners of the same English, Irish or Welshmen for the more part, or men of Calais or of the marches of the same; and that upon pain of forfeiture of the same wines so bought or sold contrary to this act, the one half of that forfeiture to be to the king's grace, and that other half to the finder of that forfeiture.

1 Henry VII c. 8. *The Statutes of the Realm*, Vol. II (1817), p. 502.

DOCUMENT 18   **FRENCH PENSIONS**

The Milanese ambassador to Ludovico Sforza, Duke of Milan.

(a) *6 December 1497*

To tell the truth, His Majesty is right in behaving well to the French, as every year he obtains 5,000 crowns from them. ... The French not only pay this sum to His Majesty, but with his knowledge and consent they give provision to the leading men of the realm, to wit, the Lord Chamberlain, Master Braiset [i.e. Bray], Master Lovel, and as these leading satraps are very rich the provision has to be very large. I hear also that they give to others, but this is not so well established as the case of these three.

(b) *17 November 1498*

I fancy also that he [Henry VII] attaches more importance to the King of France [Louis XII] than he did in the past, either from obtaining a greater sum from him, or because he values him personally more highly or from their old standing friendship when they were defending the Duchess of Brittany against France [see above, p. 83]. The peace which the Sovereigns of Spain have made with France also makes him move more cautiously. But the great pensions count more than all, which are paid by the French at this Court with the royal knowledge ... I feel sure that he will never move against France unless he sees everything upside down, and he would never wish to cause them any uneasiness unless he could do so with the utmost safety and advantage.

Calendar of State Papers and Manuscripts Existing in the Archives and Collections of Milan, Vol. I (ed. Allen B. Hinds), 1912, pp. 335 and 359–60.

DOCUMENT 19   **HENRY VII AND HENRY VI**

THE INDENTURE BETWEEN HENRY VII AND GEORGE FAWCETT, ABBOT OF WESTMINSTER, FOR THE REMOVAL OF HENRY VI FROM WINDSOR TO WESTMINSTER

Where the said King our souverain Lord to the pleasure of God and for the singuler affeccion and devocion that his grace hath to his Uncle of blessid memory King Henry the vi[th] lately begon to make and bilde of new the chapell of our Lady within the Collegeat church of Wyndesore entending to have translatid the body of his said Uncle in to the same and nygh unto him within the said chapell to have be buryed hymself. And sithens that our said souverain Lord hath ben duely enfourmed ... that for certen lawfull and resonable causis the holy body of his said Uncle King Henry the vj[th] ought to be conveyed and brought from the said Collegiat Church of Wyndesore to the said Monastery of Westm[r] and there with his fader of blessid memory King Henry the vth his moder Quene Kateryn and other his noble progenitours and auncestours sumtyme Kinges of this lond to be commytted to perpetuall sepulture. And therfor oure souverain Lord the King ... hath fynally determyned to convey and bring the said holy body of his said Uncle King Henry the vj[th] ... to the said Monastery of Westminster and there to be commytted to perpetuall sepulture in the chapel of our Lady within the church of the said Monastery – the which chapell oure said souverain Lord entendith to make and bilde of new and in the same not ferre from his said Uncle to be buried hymself.

Printed in Arthur Penrhyn Stanley, D.D., *Historical Memorials of Westminster Abbey*, 3rd and revised edn, 1869, Appendix II, IV (d), pp. 615–16.

DOCUMENT 20   **HENRY VII's WILL**

(a) And howbeit I am a sinful creature, in sin conceived, and in sin I have lived, knowing perfectly that of my merits I cannot obtain to the life everlasting, but only by the merits of thy blessed passion, and of thy infinite mercy and grace. Nevertheless my most merciful redeemer, maker and saviour, I trust by the special grace and mercy of thy most Blessed Mother ever Virgin, our Lady Saint Mary, in whom after thee in this mortal life, hath ever been my most singular trust and confidence, to whom in all my necessities I have made my continual refuge, and by whom I have hitherto in all mine adversities, ever had my special comfort and relief, will now in my most extreme need, of her infinite pity take my soul into her hands, and it present unto her most dear Son: Whereof sweetest Lady of mercy, very Mother and Virgin, well of pity, and surest refuge of all needful; most humbly, most entirely, and most heartily I beseech thee.

(b) Also we give and bequeath to the Altar within the grate [i.e. screen] of our said Tombe, our great piece of the holy Cross, which by the high provision of our Lord God, was conveyed, brought and delivered to us, from the Isle of Cyo in Greece, set in gold and garnished with pearls and precious stones; and also the precious Relic of one of the legs of Saint George, set in silver parcel gilt, which came to the hands of our Brother and Cousin Lewis of France, the time that he won and recovered the City of Milan, and given and sent to us by our Cousin the Cardinal of Amboise Legate in France: the which piece of the holy Cross, and leg of Saint George, we will be set upon the said Altar for the garnishing of the same, upon all principal and solemn feasts.

Will of King Henry VII, [16], pp. 2 and 33–4.

CHRONOLOGICAL SUMMARY

1457   28 January, Henry born at Pembroke Castle.

1461   Edward IV defeats and deposes Henry VI and claims throne.

1469   Marriage of Ferdinand, King of Aragon, to Isabella, Queen of Castile.

1470   Restoration of Henry VI.

1471   Edward IV recovers throne.
Death of Henry VI and Edward, Prince of Wales.
Henry goes into exile in Brittany.

1477   Death of Charles the Bold, Duke of Burgundy.

1483   Death of Edward IV; accession of Richard III.
Probable death of Edward V and his half-brother Richard, Duke of York.
Buckingham's rebellion.
Henry begins to style himself king.
Death of Louis XI of France; accession of Charles VIII.

1484   Henry leaves Brittany for France.

1485   7 August, Henry lands at Milford Haven.
22 August, Battle of Bosworth.
September, Henry enters London.
October, coronation.
November, meeting of first Parliament; passage of first Navigation Act.

1486   Anglo-French commercial treaty.
January, Henry marries Elizabeth of York.
March, Lovell's conspiracy.
July, three-year truce with Scotland after the Scots recapture Dunbar.
September, birth of Prince Arthur.
Simnel appears in Ireland.

1487   May, French invade Brittany.
        May, Simnel crowned as 'Edward VI' in Dublin.
        June, Battle of Stoke.
        November, Henry's second Parliament.

1488   January, treaties concluded with Maximilian.
        June, James III of Scotland defeated and killed at Battle of
            Sauchieburn; accession of James IV.
        June, defeat of Breton army at Battle of St Aubin du Cormier.
        July, Sir Richard Edgecumbe despatched to Dublin.
        August, Anne of Brittany signs Treaty of Sablé with France.
        November, Great Council summoned.

1489   January, Henry's third Parliament votes war funds; passes second
            Navigation Act.
        February, Henry concludes Treaty of Dordrecht with Burgundy
            and Treaty of Redon with Brittany.
        March, Henry concludes Treaty of Medina del Campo with Spain.
        April, assassination of Earl of Northumberland.
        April, Henry despatches an army to Brittany.
        June, Battle of Dixmunde: Henry's forces relieve West Flanders.
        July, Maximilian signs Treaty of Dordrecht with France.
        October, final defeat of Breton army.

1490   January, renewal of Anglo-Danish commercial treaty.
        Commercial treaty with Florence.

1491   May, Henry summons a Great Council.
        October, Henry's fourth Parliament.
        November, Warbeck spotted in Cork by Yorkist conspirators.
        December, Charles VIII marries Anne of Brittany.
        December, Henry sends small army to Ireland.

1492   Spain conquers Granada.
        Columbus discovers America.
        June, Kildare removed from office.
        August, Henry's conspiracy with dissident Breton nobles betrayed.
        October, Henry lands in France.
        November, Treaty of Etaples between England and France.

1493   August, death of Emperor Frederick III; accession of Maximilian I.
        Philip of Burgundy takes over effective rule of Netherlands.
        Henry imposes embargo on Anglo-Flemish trade.
        Attack on the Steelyard.
        Nine-year truce between England and Scotland.

1494   September, Charles VIII invades Italy.
       September, Henry despatches Poynings with an army to Ireland.
       December, Irish Parliament passes Poynings' Law.

1495   February, Kildare arrested; Poynings abandons expedition to
       Ulster.
       February, Sir William Stanley executed.
       March, formation of League of Venice after French enter Naples.
       July, Warbeck lands troops at Deal.
       October, Henry's fifth Parliament.
       November, Charles VIII leaves Italy.

1494   February, *Magnus Intercursus*.
       June, Kildare reinstated as Lord Deputy.
       July, Henry joins Holy League (former League of Venice).
       September, James IV of Scotland and Warbeck invade England.
       October, Henry summons a Great Council.
       October, Philip of Burgundy marries Joanna.

1497   Anglo-French treaty of commerce.
       Cabot discovers Newfoundland.
       Vasco da Gama rounds Cape.
       January, Henry's sixth Parliament.
       June, Western rebels defeated at Blackheath.
       July, Warbeck reappears in Ireland, and with the Earl of Desmond
       lays siege to Waterford.
       September, Waterford relieved by Poynings; Warbeck lands in
       Cornwall, besieges Exeter and is captured.
       September, Truce of Ayton between England and Scotland.
       December, destruction by fire of Henry's palace at Sheen.

1498   Vasco da Gama reaches India.
       Columbus discovers South American mainland.
       April, death of Charles VIII of France and accession of Louis XII.
       July, renewal of Treaty of Etaples.
       August, commercial treaty with France.

1499   Commercial treaty with Riga.
       September, Louis XII occupies Milan.
       November, execution of Warbeck and Warwick.

1500   Death of Henry's youngest son, Prince Edmund.

1501   Flight of Edmund de la Pole, Earl of Suffolk.
       November, marriage of Prince Arthur and Catherine of Aragon.

1502   February, Treaty of Perpetual Peace between England and
         Scotland.
         April, death of Prince Arthur.

1503   Spanish drive out French from Naples.
         Work starts on Henry VII Chapel in Westminster Abbey.
         February, death of Elizabeth of York.
         August, marriage of James IV of Scotland to Princess Margaret.

1504   France abandons claims on Naples.
         Henry imposes embargo on Anglo-Flemish trade.
         January, Henry's seventh and last Parliament.
         November, death of Isabella, Queen of Castile.

1505   October, Treaty of Blois between Burgundy and France.

1506   January, Philip and Joanna in England; *Malus Intercursus*;
         surrender of Suffolk arranged.
         September, death of Philip.

1508   December, League of Cambrai.
         Proxy marriage of future Charles V to Princess Mary.

1509   April 21, death of Henry VII at Richmond Palace.

LANCASTRIANS, YORKISTS AND TUDORS

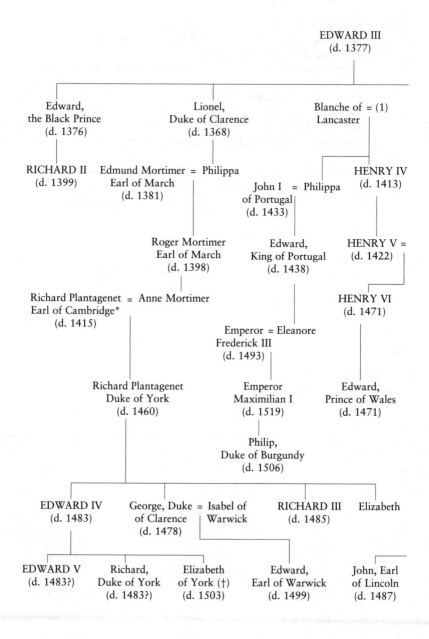

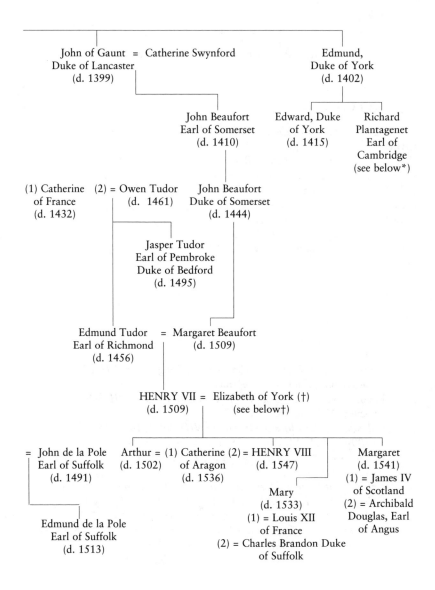

BIBLIOGRAPHY

Unless otherwise stated, the place of publication is London.

ABBREVIATIONS

B.I.H.R.	*Bulletin of the Institute of Historical Research*
C.U.P.	Cambridge University Press
E.H.R.	*English Historical Review*
Econ.H.R.	*Economic History Review*
H.M.S.O.	His (Her) Majesty's Stationery Office
J.E.H.	*Journal of Ecclesiastical History*
O.U.P.	Oxford University Press
R.H.S.	Royal Historical Society
T.R.H.S.	*Transactions of the R.H.S.*

PRIMARY SOURCES

1   Arthurson, Ian (ed.), *Documents of the Reign of Henry VII*, C.U.P., 1989.

2   Bacon, Francis, *History of the Reign of King Henry VII*, ed. J. Rawson Lumby, C.U.P., 1881.

3   Bayne, C.G., *Select Cases in the Council of Henry VII*, Selden Society, Vol. 75, 1958.

4   *Calendar of the Close Rolls. Henry VII*, Vol. I, *1485–1500*, Vol. II, *1500–1509*, H.M.S.O., 1955, 1963.

5   *Calendar of Inquisitions Post-Mortem. Henry VII*, 3 vols, H.M.S.O., 1898, 1915, 1955.

6   *Calendar of Letters, Despatches and State Papers relating to the Negotiations between England and Spain*, Vol. I. *Henry VII 1485–1509*, ed. G.A. Bergenroth, H.M.S.O., 1862.

7   *Calendar of State Papers and Manuscripts relating to English Affairs existing in the Archives and collections of Venice*, Vol. I, *1202–1509*, ed. Rawdon Brown, H.M.S.O., 1864.

8   Dudley, Edmund, *The Tree of Commonwealth*, ed. D.M. Brodie, C.U.P., 1948.
9   Elton, G.R., *The Tudor Constitution*, 2nd edn, C.U.P., 1982.
10   Fabian, Robert, *The Great Chronicle of London*, ed. A.D. Thomas and I.D. Thornley, Guildhall Library, 1939.
11   Fortescue, Sir John, *The Governance of England*, ed. Charles Plummer, O.U.P., 1885.
12   Pollard, A.F., *The Reign of Henry VII from Contemporary Sources*, 3 vols, Longman, 1913–14.
13   Roper, William, 'The Life of Sir Thomas More', in Sir Thomas More, *Utopia*, ed. J. Rawson Lumby, C.U.P., 1879.
14   Tawney, R.H. and Power, Eileen, *Tudor Economic Documents*, 3 vols, Longman, 1924.
15   Vergil, Polydore, *The Anglica Historia 1485–1537*, ed. and trans. Denys Hay, Camden Series, Vol. 74, R.H.S., 1950.
16   *Will of King Henry VII, The*, 1775.
17   Williams, C.H. (ed.), *English Historical Documents*, Vol. V, *1485–1558*, Eyre and Spottiswoode, 1967.

SECONDARY SOURCES

General

18   Alexander, Michael van Cleave, *The First of the Tudors: A Study of Henry VII and his Reign*, Croome Helm, 1981.
19   Anglo, S., *Spectacle, Pageantry and the Early Tudor Polity*, O.U.P., 1969.
20   Chrimes, S.B., *Henry VII*, Eyre Methuen, 1972.
21   Chrimes, S.B., 'The Reign of Henry VII: Some Recent Contributions', *Welsh History Review* 10, 1981.
22   Chrimes, S.B., Ross, C.D. and Griffiths, R.A., *Fifteenth-Century England 1399–1509*, Manchester University Press, 1972.
23   Colvin, Howard (ed.), *The History of the King's Works*, Vols III and IV, *1485–1660*, H.M.S.O., 1975, 1982.
24   Goodman, Anthony, *The New Monarchy: England 1471–1534*, Historical Association Studies, Blackwell, Oxford, 1988.
25   Grant, Alexander, *Henry VII: The Importance of his Reign in English History*, Lancaster Pamphlets, Methuen, 1985.
26   Jones, Michael K. and Underwood, Malcolm G., *The King's Mother: Lady Margaret Beaufort, Countess of Richmond and Derby*, C.U.P., 1992.
27   Lander, J.R., *Crown and Nobility 1450–1509*, Edward Arnold, 1976.
28   Lander, J.R., *Government and Community: England 1450–1509*, Edward Arnold, 1980.

29   Rogers, Caroline, *Henry VII*, Access to History, Hodder and
     Stoughton, 1991.
30   Wolffe, B.P., *Yorkist and Early Tudor Government, 1461–1509*,
     Historical Association 'Aids for Teachers' series, No. 12, 1966.

The Yorkist Inheritance

31   Cook, David R., *Lancastrians and Yorkists: The Wars of the Roses*,
     Seminar Studies in History, Longman,1984.
32   Dockray, Keith, 'The Political Legacy of Richard III in Northern
     England' in Griffiths, R.A. and Sherborne, J.W. (eds), *Kings and
     Nobles in the Later Middle Ages*, Alan Sutton, Gloucester, 1986.
33   Goodman, Anthony, *The Wars of the Roses: Military Activity and
     English Society 1452–97*, Routledge and Kegan Paul, 1981.
34   Ross, Charles, *Edward IV*, Eyre Methuen, 1974.
35   Ross, Charles, *Richard III*, Eyre Methuen, 1981.

The New King

36   Antonovics, A.V., 'Henry VII, King of England, "By the Grace of
     Charles VIII of France" ' in Griffiths, R.A. and Sherborne, J.W.
     (eds), *Kings and Nobles in the Later Middle Ages*, Alan Sutton,
     Gloucester, 1986.
37   Arthurson, Ian and Kingswell, Nicholas, 'The Proclamation of Henry
     Tudor as King of England, 3 November 1483', *Historical Research*
     63, 1990.
38   Carpenter, Christine, 'Henry VII and the English Polity' in
     Thompson, Benjamin (ed.), *The Reign of Henry VII: Proceedings of
     the 1993 Harlaxton Symposium*, Paul Watkins, Stamford, 1995.
39   Davies, C.S.L., 'Henry Tudor and Henry VII', *History Sixth* 1, 1987.
40   Griffiths, R.A., 'Henry Tudor: The Training of a King', *Huntington
     Library Quarterly* 49, 1986.
41   Kipling, Gordon, 'Henry VII and the Origins of Tudor Patronage' in
     Lytle, G.F. and Orgel, S. (eds), *Patronage in the Renaissance*,
     Princeton University Press, 1981.
42   Richmond, Colin, '1485 and All That, or what was going on at the
     Battle of Bosworth?' in Hammond, P.W. (ed.), *Richard III: Loyalty,
     Lordship and Law*, Richard III and Yorkist History Trust, Sutton,
     1986.

The Royal Finances

43   Alsop, J.D., 'The Exchequer in Late Medieval Government
     c. 1485–1530' in Rowe, J.G. (ed.), *Aspects of Late Medieval
     Government and Society: Essays Presented to J.R. Lander*,
     University of Toronto Press, 1986.

44   Batho, Gordon, 'The Golden Age of the Crown Estate, 1461–1509'
      in [137].
45   Bush, Michael, 'Tax Reform and Rebellion in Early Tudor England',
      History 76, 1991.
46   Challis, C.E., *The Tudor Coinage*, Manchester University Press, 1978.
47   Currin, John M., ' "Pro Expensis Ambassatorum": Diplomacy and
      Financial Administration in the Reign of Henry VII', *E.H.R.* 108,
      1993.
48   Guy, J.A., 'A Conciliar Court of Audit at Work in the Last Months
      of the Reign of Henry VII', *B.I.H.R.* 49, 1976.
49   Harriss, G.L., 'Aids, Loans and Benevolences', *Historical Journal* 6,
      1963.
50   Richardson, W.C., 'The Surveyor of the King's Prerogative', *E.H.R.*
      56, 1941.
51   Richardson, W.C., *Tudor Chamber Administration 1485–1547*,
      Louisiana State University Press, Baton Rouge, 1952.
52   Scarisbrick, J.J., 'Clerical Taxation in England, 1485–1547', *J.E.H.*
      11, 1960.
53   Starkey, David, 'After the "Revolution" ' in Coleman, Christopher
      and Starkey, David (eds), *Revolution Reassessed*, Clarendon Press,
      Oxford, 1986.
54   Wolffe, B.P., 'Henry VII's Land Revenues and Chamber Finance',
      E.H.R. 79, 1964.
55   Wolffe, B.P., *The Crown Lands 1461 to 1536. An Aspect of Yorkist
      and Early Tudor Government*, Allen and Unwin, 1970.
56   Wolffe, B.P., *The Royal Demesne in English History. The Crown
      Estate in the Governance of the Realm from the Conquest to 1509*,
      Allen and Unwin, 1971.

Central Government

The Council

57   Condon, M.M., 'An Anachronism with Intent? Henry VII's Council
      Ordinance of 1491–92' in Griffiths, R.A. and Sherborne, J.W. (eds),
      Kings and Nobles in the Later Middle Ages, Alan Sutton,
      Gloucester, 1986.
58   Condon, Margaret, 'From "Caitiff and Villain" to *Pater Patriae*:
      Reynold Bray and the Profits of Office' in Hicks, Michael (ed.),
      Profit, Piety and the Professions in Later Medieval England, Alan
      Sutton, Gloucester, 1990.
59   Guy, J.A., 'The Early-Tudor Star Chamber' in Jenkins, D. (ed.), *Legal
      History Studies*, University of Wales Press, Cardiff, 1975.
60   Guy, J.A., *The Cardinal's Court: The Impact of Thomas Wolsey in
      Star Chamber*, Harvester Press, Hemel Hempstead, 1977.

61   Heinze, R.W., *The Proclamations of the Tudor Kings*, C.U.P., 1976.
62   Lehmberg, S.E., 'Star Chamber 1485–1509', *Huntington Library Quarterly* 24, 1961.
63   Storey, R.L., 'Gentlemen-Bureaucrats' in Clough, C.H. (ed.), *Profession, Vocation and Culture in Later Medieval England*, Liverpool University Press, 1982.
64   Virgoe, R., 'Sir John Risley (1443–1512), Courtier and Councillor', *Norfolk Archaeology* 28, 1982.

The Council Learned

65   Brodie, D.M., 'Edmund Dudley, Minister of Henry VII', *T.R.H.S.* 15, 4th series, 1932.
66   Horowitz, Mark R., 'Richard Empson, Minister of Henry VII', *B.I.H.R. 55*, 1982.
67   Somerville, R., 'Henry VII's Council Learned in the Law', *E.H.R.* 54, 1939.

The Court

68   Gunn, S.J., 'The Courtiers of Henry VII', *E.H.R.* 108, 1993.
69   Starkey, David, 'Intimacy and Innovation: The Rise of the Privy Chamber, 1485–1547' in Starkey, David (ed.), *The English Court: From the Wars of the Roses to the Civil War*, Longman, 1987.

The Law

70   Baker, J.H., Introduction to *The Reports of Sir John Spelman*, Vol. II, Selden Society, 1978.
71   Blatcher, Margaret, *The Court of King's Bench 1450–1550*, Athlone Press, 1978.
72   Cameron, A., 'The Giving of Livery and Retaining in Henry VII's Reign', *Renaissance and Modern Studies* 18, 1974.
73   Dunham, W.H. Jnr., *Lord Hastings' Indentured Retainers 1461–1483; The Lawfulness of Livery and Retaining under the Yorkists and Tudors*, Transactions of the Connecticut Academy of Arts and Sciences, Vol. 39, Yale University Press, New Haven, 1955.
74   Guth, DeLoyd-J., 'Enforcing Late Medieval Law: Patterns in Litigation during Henry VII's Reign' in Baker, J.H. (ed.), *Legal Records and the Historian*, R.H.S., 1978.
75   Ives, E.W., 'The Common Lawyers in Pre-Reformation England', *T.R.H.S.* 18, 5th series, 1968.
76   Pronay, Nicholas, 'The Chancellor, the Chancery and the Council at the End of the Fifteenth Century' in Hearder, H. and Loyn, H.R. (eds), *British Government and Administration*, University of Wales Press, Cardiff, 1974.

Regional Government

77   Arthurson, Ian, 'The Rising of 1497: A Revolt of the Peasantry?' in
      Rosenthal, Joel and Richmond, Colin (eds), *People, Politics and
      Community in the Later Middle Ages*, Alan Sutton, Gloucester,
      1987.
78   Brooks, F.W., *The Council of the North*, Historical Association
      pamphlet G.25, 1966.
79   Carpenter, Christine, *Locality and Polity: A Study of Warwickshire
      Landed Society 1401–1499*, C.U.P., 1992.
80   Davies, C.S.L., 'The Crofts: Creation and Defence of a Family
      Enterprise under the Yorkists and Henry VII', *Historical Research*
      68, 1995.
81   Fletcher, Anthony, *Tudor Rebellions*, Seminar Studies in History, 3rd
      edn, Longman, 1983.
82   Luckett, D., 'Patronage, Violence and Revolt in the Reign of Henry
      VII' in Archer, Rowena E. (ed.), *Crown, Government and People in
      the Fifteenth Century*, Alan Sutton, Gloucester, 1995.
83   Pollard, A.J., *North-Eastern England during the Wars of the Roses:
      Lay Society, War and Politics 1450–1500*, Clarendon Press,
      Oxford, 1990.
84   Richmond, Colin (ed.), *People, Politics and Community in the Later
      Middle Ages,* Alan Sutton, Gloucester, 1987.
85   Williams, Glanmor, *Recovery, Reorientation and Reformation. Wales
      c. 1415–1642*, Clarendon Press, Oxford, 1987.

The Role of the Nobility

86   Bennett, Michael J., 'Henry VII and the Northern Rising of 1489',
      E.H.R. 105, 1990.
87   Cameron, A., 'A Nottinghamshire Quarrel in the Reign of Henry
      VII', *B.I.H.R.* 45, 1972.
88   Condon, Margaret, 'Ruling Elites in the Reign of Henry VII' in Ross,
      Charles (ed.), *Patronage, Pedigree and Power in Later Medieval
      England*, Alan Sutton, Gloucester, 1979.
89   Hicks, M.A., 'Dynastic Change and Northern Society: The Career of
      the 4th Earl of Northumberland 1470–89', *Northern History* 14,
      1978.
90   Jones, Michael K., 'Sir William Stanley of Holt: Politics and Family
      Allegiance in the Late Fifteenth Century', *Welsh History Review* 14,
      1989.
91   Luckett, D.A., 'The Thames Valley Conspiracies against Henry VII',
      Historical Research 68, 1995.
92   Luckett, D.A., 'Crown Patronage and Political Morality in Early
      Tudor England: The Case of Giles, Lord Daubeney', *E.H.R.* 110,
      1995.

93   Pugh, T.B., 'Henry VII and the English Nobility' in Bernard, G.W.
     (ed.), *The Tudor Nobility*, Manchester University Press, 1992.
94   Virgoe, R., 'The Recovery of the Howards in East Anglia 1485 to
     1529' in Ives, E.W., Knecht, R.J. and Scarisbrick, J.J. (eds), *Wealth
     and Power in Tudor England*, Athlone Press, 1978.
95   Weiss, Michael, 'A Power in the North? The Percies in the Fifteenth
     Century', *Northern History* 19, 1976.

Ireland

96   Bradshaw, Brendan, *The Irish Constitutional Revolution of the
     Sixteenth Century*, C.U.P., 1979.
97   Cosgrove, Art (ed.), *A New History of Ireland*. Vol. II *Medieval
     Ireland, 1169–1534*, Clarendon Press, Oxford, 1987.
98   Ellis, S.G., 'Tudor Policy and the Kildare Ascendancy in the Lordship
     of Ireland 1496–1534', *Irish Historical Review* 20, 1977.
99   Ellis, S.G., 'Henry VII and Ireland 1491–96' in Lydon, J.F. (ed.),
     England and Ireland in the Later Middle Ages, Irish Academic
     Press, Dublin, 1981.
100 Ellis, Steven G., *Tudor Ireland: Crown, Community and the Conflict
     of Cultures 1470–1603*, Longman, 1985.
101 Palmer, W., *The Problem of Ireland in Tudor Foreign Policy
     1485–1603*, Boydell Press, Woodbridge, 1994.

Great Councils and Parliaments

102 Elton, G.R., *Studies in Tudor and Stuart Politics and Government*,
     C.U.P., Vols I and II, 1974, Vol. III, 1983, Vol. IV, 1992.
103 Elton, G.R., 'The Rolls of Parliament 1449–1547', *Historical
     Journal* 22, 1979.
104 Hicks, Michael, 'Attainder, Resumption and Coercion 1461–1529',
     Parliamentary History 3, 1984.
105 Holmes, Peter, 'The Great Council in the Reign of Henry VII',
     E.H.R. 101, 1986.
106 Myers, A.R., 'Parliament 1422–1509' in Davies, R.G. and Denton
     J.H. (eds), *The English Parliament in the Middle Ages*, Manchester
     University Press, 1981.

The Church

107 Bowker, Margaret, *The Secular Clergy in the Diocese of Lincoln
     1495–1520*, C.U.P., 1968.
108 Brown, Keith, 'Wolsey and Ecclesiastical Order: The Case of the
     Franciscan Observants' in Gunn, S.J. and Lindley, P.G. (eds),
     Cardinal Wolsey: Church, State and Art, C.U.P., 1991.
109 Cross, Claire, *Church and People 1450–1660*, Fontana, 1976.

110 Davies, C.S.L., 'Bishop John Morton, the Holy See, and the Accession of Henry VII', *E.H.R.* 102, 1987.
111 Goodman, A., 'Henry VII and Christian Renewal' in Robbins, Keith (ed.), *Studies in Church History*, Vol. 17, *Religion and Humanism*, Blackwell, Oxford, 1981.
112 Harper-Bill, Christopher, 'Archbishop John Morton and the Province of Canterbury 1486–1500', *J.E.H.* 29, 1978.
113 Harper-Bill, Christopher, *The Pre–Reformation Church in England 1400–1530*, Seminar Studies in History, Revised edn, Longman, 1996.
114 Kaufman, P.I., 'Henry VII and Sanctuary', *Church History* 53, 1984.
115 Knowles, Dom David, *The Religious Orders in England*, Vol. III, *The Tudor Age*, C.U.P., 1961.
116 Swanson, R.N., *Church and Society in Late Medieval England*, O.U.P., 1989.
117 Thomson, J.A.F., 'Piety and Charity in Late Medieval London', *J.E.H.* 16, 1965.
118 Thomson, John A.F., *The Early Tudor Church and Society, 1485–1529*, Longman, 1993.
119 Underwood, M.G., 'Politics and Piety in the Household of Lady Margaret Beaufort', *J.E.H.* 38, 1987.
120 Wilkie, W.E., *The Cardinal Protectors of England: Rome and the Tudors before the Reformation*, C.U.P., 1974.

The Economy

121 Awty, Brian G., 'Henry VII's First Attempt to Exploit Iron in Ashdown Forest', *Bulletin of the Wealden Iron Research Group* 11, 2nd series, 1991.
122 Beresford, M.W., *Deserted Medieval Villages*, Lutterworth Press, 1971.
123 Beresford, M.W. and St Joseph, J.K., *Medieval England. An Aerial Survey*, C.U.P., 2nd edn, 1979.
124 Blanchard, Ian, 'Population Change, Enclosure, and the Early Tudor Economy', *Econ.H.R.* 23, 1970.
125 Bridbury, A.R., 'Sixteenth-century Farming', *Econ.H.R.* 27, 1974.
126 Clark, Peter and Slack, Paul, *English Towns in Transition 1500–1700*, O.U.P., 1976.
127 Coleman, D.C., *The Economy of England 1450–1750*, O.U.P., 1977.
128 Dyer, Christopher, 'Deserted Medieval Villages in the West Midlands', *Econ.H.R.* 35, 1982.
129 Gottfried, R.S., 'Population, Plague, and the Sweating Sickness: Demographic Movements in Late Fifteenth-century England', *Journal of British Studies* 17, 1977.
130 Hoskins, W.G., 'Harvest Fluctuations and English Economic History 1480–1619', *Agricultural History Review* 12, 1964.

131   Kermode, Jennifer I., 'Urban Decline? The Flight from Office in Late Medieval York', *Econ.H.R.* 35, 1982.

132   Lacey, Kay, 'The Military Organisation of the Reign of Henry VII', unpublished paper given at the 1995 Harlaxton Conference on Chivalry and Warfare.

133   Loades, David, *The Tudor Navy: An Administrative, Political and Military History*, Scolar Press, Aldershot, 1992.

134   Palliser, D.M., 'A Crisis in English Towns? The Case of York 1460–1640', *Northern History* 14, 1978.

135   Ramsay, G.D., *English Overseas Trade during the Centuries of Emergence*, Macmillan, 1957.

136   Ramsey, Peter, 'Overseas Trade in the Reign of Henry VII: The Evidence of the Customs Accounts', *Econ.H.R.* 6, 1963.

137   Thirsk, Joan (ed.), *The Agrarian History of England and Wales*, Vol. IV, *1500–1640*, C.U.P., 1967.

Foreign Policy

138   Bridge, John S.C., *A History of France from the Death of Louis XI. Vol. I, Reign of Charles VIII, Regency of Anne of Beaujeu, 1483–1493*, Clarendon Press, Oxford, 1921.

139   Currin, John M., 'Pierre Le Pennec, Henry VII of England, and the Breton Plot of 1492: A Case Study in Diplomatic Pathology', *Albion* 23, 1991.

140   Doran, Susan, *England and Europe 1485–1603*, Seminar Studies in History, 2nd edn, Longman, 1996.

141   Lloyd, T.H., *England and the German Hanse, 1157–1611: A Study of their Trade and Commercial Diplomacy*, C.U.P., 1991.

142   Weightman, Christine, *Margaret of York, Duchess of Burgundy, 1446–1503*, Alan Sutton, Gloucester, 1989.

Scotland

143   Arthurson, Ian. 'The King's Voyage into Scotland: the War that Never Was' in Williams, Daniel (ed.), *England in the Fifteenth Century*, Boydell Press, Woodbridge, 1987.

144   MacDougall, Norman, *James III: A Political Study*, John Donald, Edinburgh, 1982.

145   MacDougall, Norman, *James IV*, John Donald, Edinburgh, 1989.

146   Nicholson, Ranald, *Scotland: The Later Middle Ages*. Vol. 2. Oliver and Boyd, Edinburgh, 1974.

INDEX

Seminar Studies in History
General Editors: Clive Emsley & Gordon Martel

The series was founded by Patrick Richardson in 1966. Between 1980 and 1996 Roger Lockyer edited the series before handing over to Clive Emsley (Professor of History at the Open University) and Gordon Martel (Professor of International History at the University of Northern British Columbia, Canada and Senior Research Fellow at De Montfort University).

Medieval England
The Pre-Reformation Church in England 1400–1530 (Revised edition)
   Christopher Harper-Bill   0 582 28989 0
Lancastrians and Yorkists: The Wars of the Roses
   David R Cook   0 582 35384 X

Tudor England
Henry VII (Third edition)
   Roger Lockyer &
   Andrew Thrush   0 582 20912 9
Henry VIII (Second edition)
   M D Palmer   0 582 35437 4
Tudor Rebellions (Fourth edition)
   Anthony Fletcher &
   Diarmaid MacCulloch   0 582 28990 4
The Reign of Mary I (Second edition)
   Robert Tittler   0 582 06107 5
Early Tudor Parliaments
   Michael A R Graves   0 582 03497 3
The English Reformation 1530–1570
   W J Sheils   0 582 35398 X
Elizabethan Parliaments 1559–1601 (Second edition)
   Michael A R Graves   0 582 29196 8
England and Europe 1485–1603 (Second edition)
   Susan Doran   0 582 28991 2
The Church of England 1570–1640
   Andrew Foster   0 582 35574 5

Stuart Britain
Social Change and Continuity in Early Modern England 1590–1750
   Barry Coward   0 582 35453 6
James I (Second edition)
   S J Houston   0 582 20911 0
The English Civil War
   Martyn Bennett   0 582 35392 0
Charles I
   Brian Quintrell   0 582 00354 7
The English Republic 1649–1660
   Toby Barnard   0 582 35231 2
Radical Puritans in England 1550–1660
   R J Acheson   0 582 35515 X
The Restoration and the England of Charles II (Second edition)
   John Miller   0 582 29223 9
The Glorious Revolution (Second edition)
   John Miller   0 582 29222 0
The Financial Revolution 1660–1760
   Henry Roseveare   0 582 35449 8

Early Modern Europe
The Renaissance
   Alison Brown   0 582 35383 1
The Emperor Charles V
   Martin Rady   0 582 35475 7
French Renaissance Monarchy: Francis I and Henry II (Second edition)
   Robert Knecht   0 582 28707 3
The Protestant Reformation in Europe
   Andrew Johnston   0 582 07020 1
The French Wars of Religion 1559–1598 (Second edition)
   Robert Knecht   0 582 28533 X
The Dutch Revolt 1559–1648
   Peter Limm   0 582 35594 X
Phillip II
   Geoffrey Woodward   0 582 07232 8
The Thirty Years' War
   Peter Limm   0 582 35373 4
Louis XIV
   Peter Campbell   0 582 01770 X
Spain in the Seventeenth Century
   Graham Darby   0 582 07234 4
Peter the Great
   William Marshall   0 582 00355 5

Europe 1789–1918
Revolution and Terror in France 1789–1795 (Second edition)
   D G Wright   0 582 00379 2
Napoleon and Europe
   D G Wright   0 582 35457 9
The Eastern Question 1774–1923 (Revised edition)
   A L Macfie   0 582 29195 X
The 1848 Revolutions (Second edition)
   Peter Jones   0 582 06106 7
Bismarck & Germany 1862–1890
   D G Williamson   0 582 35413 7
Imperial Germany 1890–1918
   Ian Porter & Ian Armour   0 582 03496 5
The Dissolution of the Austro-Hungarian Empire (Second edition)
   John W Mason   0 582 29466 5
Second Empire and Commune: France 1848–1871 (Second edition)
   William H C Smith   0 582 28705 7
France 1870–1914 (Second edition)
   Robert Gildea   0 582 29221 2
The Scramble for Africa
   M E Chamberlain   0 582 35204 5

Cont.

Seminar Studies in History
General Editors: Clive Emsley & Gordon Martel